LOCAL GOVERNMENT IN *California*

LOCAL GOVERNMENT
IN *California*

JOHN C. BOLLENS

STANLEY SCOTT

UNIVERSITY OF CALIFORNIA PRESS
BERKELEY AND LOS ANGELES   1951

UNIVERSITY OF CALIFORNIA PRESS
BERKELEY AND LOS ANGELES, CALIFORNIA
CAMBRIDGE UNIVERSITY PRESS, LONDON, ENGLAND
COPYRIGHT, 1951, BY
THE REGENTS OF THE UNIVERSITY OF CALIFORNIA

Preface

The growing awareness of the significance of local government and the increased willingness to face problems and to take action, evidenced by many diverse groups, have prompted the authors to bring together in this volume a fund of information concerning primary governmental units on the California scene. The variations of local organizational structure and of administrative responsibilities are examined, along with the related import of home rule. The local duties performed, their relative importance in terms of cost, and the sources of supporting revenue are outlined. Special consideration is given to the unsolved problems of providing services for unincorporated areas and of coördinating administration in metropolitan regions.

This study was conceived and in large part carried out as a phase of the research program maintained by the Bureau of Public Administration, University of California, Berkeley. Particularly helpful to the authors were the encouragement and unflagging interest of Professor Samuel C. May, Director, Mrs. Mary L. Sisson, and other Bureau staff members. For reviewing various parts of the manuscript sincere appreciation is expressed to Nestor Barrett, Richard Bartle, Philip R. Berger, Garrett R. Breckenridge, Alfred H. Campion, Vincent Cooper, George Duggar, John H. England, S. Smith Griswold, Fred Grumm, William McC. Hiscock, Charles I. Schottland, John M. Selig, Herbert R. Stolz, D. M. Teeter, Sterling S. Winans, and James N. York.

J. C. B. and S. S.

Los Angeles and Berkeley
January 15, 1951

Contents

I   Status and Prospects   1
Functions and Finance · Administrative Organization · Planning · Home Rule · Associations of Local Government Officials · Local Areas

II   City Organization and Governmental Forms   12
Special Charter Organization · General Law Organization · Freeholder Charter Organization · Mayor-Council Form · Commission Form · Council-Manager Form

III   City Functions and Finance   29
General Government · Protection to Persons and Property · Public Works · Municipally Owned Public Service Enterprises · Charities and Corrections · Health · Education · Recreation · Finance

IV   Adjustment of City Areas   51
Fringe Areas · Metropolitan Areas

V   County Governmental Organization   70
General Law Counties · Charter Counties · City and County of San Francisco

Contents   vii

VI   County Functions and Finance   94
       General Government · Protection to Persons and Property · Charities and Corrections · Highways · Health and Sanitation · Education · Recreation · Finance

VII   Special Districts: Characteristics and Patterns   119
       Organization Procedures and Governing Boards · Powers, Changes in Area, and Dissolution · Supervision and Coöperation with Other Governments · Agricultural Districts · School Districts · Quasi-Municipal Districts · Metropolitan Districts

Bibliography   144

Index   147

Tables

1	California Local Charter Cities	18
2	California Charter and General Law Cities Appointing City Managers or Chief Administrative Officers	25
3	California and U.S. Council-Manager Cities of More than 1,000 Population, December, 1949	27
4	California Cities: Local Non-Property Sources of Revenue	48
5	California Cities: Expenditure of Revenue Collected Directly	50
6	California Cities: Average Areas and Percentage Distributions by Area and Population Class	53
7	General Law Counties: Mandatory Appointed Officers and Boards	72
8	General Law Counties: Consolidation of Offices	76
9	San Francisco Officials and Agencies Appointed by and Operating under the Mayor	90
10	San Francisco Officials and Agencies Operating under the Chief Administrative Officer	92
11	Miscellaneous San Francisco Officials and Agencies	93
12	California Counties: Expenditure of Revenue Collected Directly	117
13	Number of Active Local Governmental Taxing Units in California, by Selected Years	122

CHAPTER I

Status and Prospects

Vitality is currently the prevailing characteristic of local governments in California. Cities and counties, the two local units that were most significant in the early years, continue to be important. In more recent years they have been joined by large numbers of a third type of local government, the special-purpose district. All three units are active and influential; none is merely a relic of a former day of importance. Furthermore, the record of changes that have been made and the suggestions now pending for additional alterations and extensions indicate that these three units contain adequate resources and potentialities for the development of a sound, progressive, and flexible system of local government. The full attainment of such a goal should be a matter of considerable concern in a state faced with the constant challenge of adjustment to pressures of an increasing population.

FUNCTIONS AND FINANCE

Population growth and the need for rising levels of locally provided public services have forced local governments to expand their activities. Counties have added many functions relating to health, welfare, water conservation, flood control, and aids to agriculture. Cities on their part have responded with a wide range of activities, including parks and recreation, airports, housing, waste collection and disposal, and public-owned and operated utilities. There has been a rapid growth of single-purpose special districts which furnish services to urbanized areas not possessing municipal governments and to metropolitan areas lacking an over-all unit. As a consequence the traditional special-district functions, education and irrigation, have been joined by a long list of services including sewage disposal, fire and police protection, water supply, cemetery maintenance, highway lighting, and many others.

Concurrent with the numerical increase in local functions, there has been a decrease of differences between the three types of units.

No longer can it be said simply that counties render all rural services and cities exclusively satisfy urban needs. A much more accurate appraisal is that counties continue to dominate some functions, cities lead in certain others, and all three types, including special districts, have many similar duties. 1. A number of services are needed by rural and urban residents alike. Some of these are performed exclusively by the county for all citizens (social welfare, probation, testing of weights and measures, and recording of documents and vital information). Some are performed by the county for inhabitants of unincorporated territory and may be performed optionally by the city or the county for municipal residents (tax assessment and collection, public health, recreation, and phases of judicial administration). Others are provided by the county for unincorporated areas and by the city for municipal residents (police protection, minimum fire protection, and provision of highways and streets). One is performed for all citizens by a type of special district (public education). 2. A number of services are necessary in city or suburban areas, but are not ordinarily required by rural populations. These are supplied by the city for its own residents and by various special districts for those persons living in unincorporated suburban territory (sewage collection and disposal, water supply, street lighting, and higher levels of police and fire protection than the counties ordinarily make available). 3. Services of a peculiarly rural nature are performed either by the county (agricultural aids, and forest and wildlife protection), or by special districts (irrigation and soil conservation).

Possibly the growth of special districts, particularly those serving unincorporated urban areas, will have the effect of extending county activities further into fields ordinarily considered to be primarily municipal. Some districts are now governed directly by the county board of supervisors, and many others must have their budget approved by the board. These county powers could be developed and utilized to bring many districts into the county administrative structure. Trends in that direction are perceptible. If this should take place, the county will have approached still closer to fulfilling the duty of acting as the basic service agency in non-city areas. Certainly the failure of the traditional techniques of annexation and incorporation to keep pace with the needs of unincorporated areas emphasizes this possibility.

Another way of viewing the distribution of functions among the various local governments is in terms of comparative expenditures. Counties spend more than half their total funds of $475 million on charities and corrections, primarily the social welfare programs. Other major county expenditures include the costs of general gov-

Status and Prospects

ernment, highways, and protection to persons and property (primarily law enforcement and jail maintenance, recording, agricultural aids, and fire protection). Cities pay one-third of their outlay of about $300 million for protection to persons and property (fire and police), slightly over one-sixth for streets, and smaller portions for general government, interest and debt payments, sanitation and recreation. Many cities also emphasize public-service enterprises, including supply of water and electric power, maintenance of wharves and landings, and operation of mass-transit systems. Special-district outlays of more than $500 million are dominated by the costs of public education which constitute 90 per cent of the total. Other important special-district expenditures are for irrigation, protection to persons and property (fire protection and flood control), and health and sanitation (chiefly sewage collection and disposal).

State and federal aids are the most important sources of county revenues, providing exactly half of the total. Property taxes bring in more than 40 per cent, and other minor local sources account for the remainder. Cities are much less dependent than counties upon subventions, which provide a little more than 20 per cent of municipal revenues. The degree of dependence upon the property tax by cities and counties is about equal. Miscellaneous locally collected receipts, such as fees, licenses, permits, and sales taxes, yield the counties only small returns, but supply the cities with almost 40 per cent of their resources. Municipal public-service enterprises are financed almost wholly from their own revenues. Special districts resemble counties in their heavy reliance on subventions and property taxes which yield 38 and 52 per cent, respectively, of district revenues. A number of districts, notably those handling sewage disposal and water supply, are turning toward service charges as an additional revenue source. Irrigation districts have long used water and power sales as an important source of revenue.

There are two outstanding local finance problems in California. First is the necessity of expanding the county's local tax base so that the county may have more freedom financially to broaden its activities and meet local needs. Second are the large-scale construction requirements of school districts for new classroom facilities, of cities for streets and sewage disposal facilities, and of counties for highways. The county sales tax, as well as such other excises as the tobacco tax, has been proposed to meet the first problem. Assumption of additional responsibility by the state and/or national governments for welfare programs would relieve some of the burden now imposed on the property tax although such action would not actually broaden the county's local revenue base. Efforts to handle the second problem have already resulted in state expenditures and commitments of hundreds of millions of dollars for school, sewage disposal, and highway construction aid during the postwar years. State gasoline tax allocations to cities and counties have done much to help these units pay for their street and highway needs.

ADMINISTRATIVE ORGANIZATION

Major developments have been under way for some time in the administrative organization and techniques of many California local governmental units. Most consequential of these changes in administration is the rapidly expanding use of a professionally trained, appointed general manager of local governmental affairs. This development is best exemplified in California cities. Installation of city managers or chief administrative officers charged with the responsibility of supervising important city services is taking place at a spectacular rate, unsurpassed in any other state.

The council-manager form of government, often called the chief contribution of the United States to municipal administration, has been highly successful in improving public performance in the cities where it has been adopted. More than thirty California cities have initiated this plan within the last two years, with the result that one of every three cities in the state now employs a manager or administrative officer. In most of these cities the administrative authority resides in the manager. The council holds final legislative authority but does not engage in actual administration. The mayor usually does little more than other councilmen with the exception of presiding at council meetings. Although the manager principle has been outstandingly successful in terms of administrative efficiency, there have been complaints of a diminution of political leadership in manager cities. As a remedy the separate and direct election of the mayor has been proposed, on the theory that the additional prestige and responsibility of such an office would help to focus and facilitate the development of community leadership.

Counties have not utilized the concept of a general manager as much as cities, either in the number of such installations or in the specific authority allocated to the offices. Less than one-fifth of the counties of California possess an appointed officer supervising a number of important activities. Furthermore, only a few of these officers have been assigned responsibilities comparable in number and importance to those handled by their counterparts in city government. More meaningful than these comparisons, however, is the fact that the concept has made better progress in counties during the last

Status and Prospects

three years than in all previous years combined. Its recent adoption in both urban and rural counties which are widely separated geographically, and the variations in responsibilities assigned to the administrative officers, emphasize the flexibility of the general manager idea and lend weight to the probability that it will soon be embodied in the administrative structures of additional counties.

The managerial idea is apparent in school districts, which are the most numerous of the special districts. The concept was, in fact, first used in the local governmental system by school districts when they appointed superintendents to oversee their operations. It is not so readily noticeable in many other types of special districts, largely because of the limited scope of their activities. Unlike cities and counties, which are multipurpose, most of the districts perform only one function and have a very small administrative structure. Even so, many of the smaller districts have a part-time or full-time general administrator. Some of the larger units, such as the Metropolitan Water District of Southern California and the East Bay Municipal Utility District, have detailed administrative organizations, headed by general managers.

The managerial idea has also been influential in several local governments which do not operate under the manager form. Use of the concept is particularly vital in some of the more populous urban centers of the state. Excellent illustrations are the employment of an assistant to the mayor of San Francisco (in addition to that city-county's chief administrative officer), and the recent recommendation that a chief administrative officer be appointed to assist the mayor of Los Angeles. These examples demonstrate the increased importance attached to the critical job of coördinating administration.

Another phase of this trend toward integrated administration, and one which is necessary for the complete success of the managerial idea, is the concentration of responsibility in a few officials who can be held directly accountable to the electorate. This development has resulted in a numerical reduction of elected officials, and boards and commissions. It is evident in many council-manager cities where the elected council appoints the manager who is responsible for all administrative activities and personnel. The trend is less apparent but also present in numerous special districts and particularly in the school districts. The only elected school officials, the board of trustees, appoint a superintendent who is given considerable final authority over administrative and teaching employees. Concentration of responsibility and authority is least characteristic of counties, most of which continue to have their administrative operations distributed among a large number of independently elected officers. A major curtailment of the number of elected officials has occurred in only three counties: Los Angeles, Sacramento, and Santa Clara. Smaller decreases are also noticeable in some of the less populous counties which have consolidated several offices and thus reduced the elective total. Widespread and thoroughgoing application of the general manager principle in counties will be handicapped until there is a concentration of the diffused administrative authority.

Improved local administrative techniques in such fields as budgeting, purchasing, and personnel have also received widespread acceptance. Frequently they have materialized in connection with the two major structural changes of appointing a general administrator and electing only a small number of policy-making officials. Successful installation of these techniques, however, should not necessarily be considered dependent upon conversion to the manager form, for they are found in numerous non-manager governments. In general they are well established in many California cities and counties, particularly the larger units and those operating under their own locally drafted charters. Many special districts have also adopted some of these procedures.

PLANNING

Acceptance of the need for some kind of continuous planning activity is apparent in many cities. A similar attitude is growing among counties. The evidence regarding special districts is fragmentary but indicates that except in the cases of school, irrigation, and metropolitan districts there is probably less awareness of planning needs among districts than among cities and counties. Most of the work of city planners has stressed zoning, lot and street pattern, and other aspects of physical layout. A smaller proportion of counties participate in planning, and many of them have emphasized general economic studies which have sometimes been undertaken with the specific aim of attracting new industries. Most special districts are so small and so limited in resources that these factors alone preclude any very effective planning on an individual district basis. The large metropolitan districts, whose areas are frequently regional in character, are in a much better position to make adequate plans for future development in their own special field of operations. An increase in planning activity and a broadening of its scope, plus more adequate controls and use of the other planning tools, such as the capital-improvements budget, are necessary if local governments are to cope with the problems facing them.

HOME RULE

Changes in administrative organization and techniques have been facilitated through citizen use of state constitutional provisions relating to home rule for cities and counties. In addition to providing the means for greater administrative flexibility, the constitutional right of county and city inhabitants to draft their own charters has permitted both types of units to endow themselves with some additional functions; however, the functional gains of cities are much more evident and substantial than those of counties.

Although city home rule is extensive in scope, it is not available to all municipalities in California. Any county may draw up its own charter, but a city may not do so until it has a population of more than 3,500. The eligible cities have more actively utilized home rule; one-third of them have formulated their own charters while less than one-fifth of the counties operate under home-rule provisions. No special districts possess local charters; their powers are specifically enumerated in the state legislation that permits their creation. Since some of these laws do not outline the administrative organization in detail, however, many district governing boards are able to exercise considerable discretion in determining administrative structure.

Despite the influence of home-rule powers upon local functions and administrative organization, some of these changes are occurring in general law cities and, to a lesser extent, in general law counties. The liberality of the legislation pertaining to city governmental organization is a pertinent example. Practically all cities that function under state laws of general application rather than under their own charters are known as sixth-class cities. It is possible for them to choose either the council-manager or mayor-council form of government. Furthermore, if the voters of a sixth-class city desire to have a more closely knit, responsible administrative organization, such an alternative is available to them. Only the five members of the council must be elected, and the clerk and treasurer may be either appointed or elected at the discretion of the local voters. Other officers are appointed by the council. A wide range of functions is permitted non-charter cities under existing state laws.

Counties are more severely restricted by general state laws, largely because they are in many ways still administrative subdivisions of the state government. General law counties are required to elect many officials. Notwithstanding these legal stipulations, certain state laws and constitutional provisions enable any county to attain partial administrative reorganization. This can be done through supervisorial consolidation of specified elective positions, allocation of many new functions to the supervisors or their appointees, development of accounting, budgeting, purchasing, and other staff functions under the supervisors, and supervisorial control of most county salaries. There is no wide difference between the functions that can be exercised by general law and by charter counties.

ASSOCIATIONS OF LOCAL GOVERNMENT OFFICIALS

Various organizations of elected and appointed officials do much to further local administrative and structural reforms. Foremost among these are two which represent cities and counties. The League of California Cities is considered as outstanding among the thirty-nine state municipal leagues active in the United States. It was started more than a half century ago, and its legislative, informational, and research activities are well recognized and influential. The more recently established County Supervisors' Association of California performs related functions for the counties and is increasingly effective. Because of its services to counties, it is a unique organization within its field of operation. Most other groups are organized on a functional rather than a unit basis. The California Chapter of the American Institute of Planners, the Southern California Planning Congress, and the California State, County and Municipal Purchasing Agents' Association are three illustrations. These unit and functional groups generally affiliate with similar nationwide agencies, many of which have their headquarters at the Public Administration Clearing House in Chicago. The existence of all these organizations offers excellent opportunities for solving problems of local governmental structure, finance and administration, and there is much evidence that the means are being used advantageously.

LOCAL AREAS

A significant problem confronting local citizens and officials involves the adequacy of existing local areas. Counties are the only territorially inclusive local units. Together fifty-seven counties and one city-county constitute the entire area of the state. Cities are similar to counties in that no two municipalities may occupy the same area, but they are strikingly different in that more than three hundred of them cover only about one-hundredth of the land of California. The 4,356 special districts offer still a third variation. They embrace a major part of the entire state, but two or more of them are frequently superimposed upon each other or on one or more cities or counties. Furthermore, any one special district does not necessarily include exactly the same area as another special district, city, or county active in the same general territory. Some districts may include portions of an area which is also a segment of other districts, cities, or counties. In contrast to cities, many special districts may cross county boundaries. There is thus a bewildering array of local governmental areas which it is practically impossible to visualize because few maps indicate the size and location of all these three major types of units.

Like other western states whose early populations were sparse and highly concentrated in certain localities, California has a relatively small number of counties in proportion to its area. Many states have two to four times the number of counties. As the population of California has become more scattered, transportation and communication improvements have substantially reduced the necessity of having a great many more county units of small size. As a result, there has been only slightly more than a doubling of the original twenty-seven counties during the first hundred years of California's statehood. The last subdivision of a county was completed more than forty years ago when Imperial County was carved out of San Diego County in 1907.

Because of the relatively small number of counties, it is not surprising that there has been little interest in large-scale consolidation of such areas in California. Only a few reorganization plans have been advocated. The most recent among those was the proposal, first recommended in 1934 and repeated seven years later, to regroup counties into fifteen units. More general attention has been paid to suggestions that two specific counties be permitted to consolidate if their residents wish them to do so. Both in 1912 and in 1914 state constitutional amendments were rejected which would, if passed, have enabled the city-county of San Francisco and Alameda County to merge if the two units were mutually agreeable. A similar amendment relating to San Francisco and San Mateo County was also turned down in 1914. Since the early 1920's there has been intermittent interest in reviving San Francisco-San Mateo County consolidation but at present concern over the matter is practically nonexistent.

Detailed consideration has also been given to the idea that some or all of the cities in a single county be merged with the county. A proposal relating to all of the cities of Alameda County failed to pass in 1921. Another plan to merge the cities of Oakland, Emeryville, and Piedmont to form a new county by splitting away from Alameda County was also defeated by the local voters in the following year. This latter project was somewhat similar to the one carried out in 1856 when San Francisco succeeded in separating from the remainder of the county (which became San Mateo County) and forming the city-county of San Francisco. Territorial consolidation of the City of Los Angeles with the County of Los Angeles as well as complete separation of the city from the county have been urged from time to time.

Although existing California county areas show only a very limited relationship to economic and social unities, it seems highly unlikely that comprehensive alterations will be made in the near future. Major changes in the state constitution would be necessary, and important obstacles include the fact that counties serve as the present basis for legislative representation and as a unit of local political organization. It is much more conceivable that instead there will be a greater use of the possibilities for consolidation of *functions* among counties, or between a county and its cities, through joint administration or exchange of services.

California cities are experiencing a much more serious problem of area adjustment. Most of them are faced with safety, health, and welfare difficulties, recently created by rapid urbanization of certain sections of land lying immediately beyond their own legal limits. The cities' attempts to persuade urban fringes to annex have often proved unsuccessful. Quite frequently these fringes have not only turned down annexation offers but also have expressed no interest in incorporating as separate cities. Taking a narrow view, it is not difficult to understand the motivating cause. Fringe inhabitants are receiving numerous county-financed services which are being paid for largely by residents of the incorporated cities of the county. There is no existing state legislation requiring an area which has reached a certain population density to incorporate, to annex, or to pay its own way directly through special districts created by the county. There are indications, however, that one of these approaches for areas needing a higher level of service than that which is rendered county-wide will soon pass beyond the discussion stage.

Many cities are also part of larger metropolitan population concentrations. The six metropolitan areas in California may be commonly characterized as jumbles of tens or hundreds of cities and other local governmental units. Their problems are numerous and serious. No metropolitan area in this state or in any other state has worked out a comprehensive solution of the maze of governmental jurisdictions, almost all of which are supplying services to only a limited portion of the metropolitan population. Various remedial suggestions have been made and some progress toward integration is apparent in several of these socially and economically unified but governmentally divided regions.

Special districts present complicated area problems. Generally

Status and Prospects

they constitute attempts to satisfy a single need of a particular locality. Frequently, however, the area requesting a service varies slightly from function to function and the district pattern is one of partly overlapping governmental units. Furthermore, the area included within a particular district is often too small for the most effective and economical operation, and many districts are created without thought of their relation to or effect upon neighboring territory. The result is organization of an excessive number of local governments.

A state-wide attempt to improve this situation has been made and is continuing in the case of school districts. State agencies with definite policies for reorganization have backed local studies aimed at drastically reducing the number of independent units. Although some reorganization has resulted from this program, most recommendations have been rejected by local voters.

Certain special districts, created to solve problems over a large territory containing numerous cities and parts or all of one or more counties, indicate a real understanding of the large scope of problems confronting various sectors of the state. These large special districts are active not only in heavily urbanized areas in such matters as water supply, air pollution, sanitation, and bridge construction and operation, but also in predominately rural areas, especially in connection with irrigation. The comparative ease with which many types of districts are created and their considerable freedom of action raises certain major policy questions which have been largely untouched up to the present time. Closer control or supervision of some types of districts by the county and other types by the state seems to be needed. These changes should include provision for more careful consideration of the necessity and feasibility of organizing new districts, as well as for the definition of each district's area.

California's local government presents a varied and frequently complex scene. The problems are many, and they are difficult to solve, but significant improvements have been made. The existing local framework will persist for a long time, but its duties and its detailed workings are subject to constant modification. In this way local government is evolving into a more adequate instrument for the provision of direct public services to the people. The continuation and proper guidance of these developments is dependent, however, upon a clear citizen awareness of local problems and needs. The level of effectiveness already achieved by California's local government reflects the influence of popular understanding. A further challenge to full comprehension rests upon both private citizen and public official.

CHAPTER II

City Organization and Governmental Forms

Operating within the framework of the state constitution and laws, California cities are currently functioning under either special legislative charters, general state legislation, or local freeholder charters. Such was not always the situation even after California became a state. Before adoption of the existing constitution in 1879, sections of which made possible the beginning of comprehensive municipal home rule in California, most cities operated under special charters conferred by the state legislature. Special charter cities in existence when further adoption of such charters was prohibited in 1879 were permitted to continue under their old charters. Alviso and Gilroy are the only cities now actively operating under their pre-1879 special charters, and like all cities they are protected from additional special legislation.

SPECIAL CHARTER ORGANIZATION

In the thirty-year period of the first state constitution from 1849 to 1879, a hundred and thirty-three special charters were granted to seventy-three cities. Typical powers frequently given by the legislature to cities in these charters were to make ordinances and determine penalties for violations, prevent and remove nuisances, license and regulate various kinds of businesses, construct and maintain public buildings and areas, regulate building construction, organize and maintain a common school system, provide for city elections, borrow money, incur indebtedness, and levy taxes to a limited extent.[1]

Although items enumerated in special legislative charters were grants of power of local self-government, actual interference by the state legislature in local affairs was common rather than exceptional.

---

[1] Various phases of the evolution of municipal home rule in California are considered in detail by John C. Peppin in four articles appearing in the *California Law Review*, November, 1941; March, 1942; December, 1944; and December, 1946.

City Organization and Governmental Forms

Charters were often amended, superseded, or repealed, and other special acts substantially intervened in the activities of individual cities. Only in isolated instances were the desires of city officials or residents considered before such state actions went into effect.

There were many kinds of special state laws enacted before 1879 which interfered with municipal affairs, but they can be grouped generally into three classes. Meddling in the financial affairs of specific cities was perhaps most prevalent. Designated municipalities were ordered to pay individual claims, transfer money in city funds, issue bonds without acquiring prior approval of the local voters, pay certain salaries to city officers, spend money or levy taxes for many purposes, sell city-owned property, and receive city warrants or other claims in payment of city taxes. A second state legislative approach was to establish special boards or commissions whose representatives were not selected by the officials or residents of the city. These boards were empowered to regulate various matters of local concern, such as fire protection, municipal waterworks, parks, and streets. In the third type of intrusion the state ostensibly enabled the city to act on certain matters. This was the most deceptive form of interference since the California Supreme Court early held that many of these laws would be interpreted as being compulsory. Thus, state laws purporting to be permissive were actually mandatory and directed cities to assume additional functions.

The scope of state intervention in local matters had been substantially reduced even before restrictions were placed in the new constitution of 1879. The California Supreme Court had already completely abondoned the doctrine of absolute legislative supremacy over cities. In the four years immediately preceding the constitutional convention of 1879, the court announced three implied limitations on state legislative power over city activities: (1) no interference with city affairs by mandatory state legislation since such action violated the inherent right of local self-government; (2) no legislatively authorized claims against cities for municipal purposes without the consent of those to be taxed for such payment; and (3) no creation by the state legislature of claims which were not for municipal purposes against the funds or property of cities. The framers of the new constitution in 1879 placed into Article XI of the state constitution several provisions curtailing state legislative power over municipal affairs. The most important new sections prohibited special legislation, provided for the incorporation of cities under general law, and empowered any city of not less than 100,000 residents to construct its own charter. This latter provision was broadened in 1892 to permit a city containing more than 3,500 inhabitants to have a local charter. Subsequently through constitutional amendments in 1896 and 1914 local charter and special charter cities were given considerably more freedom from legislative control of their municipal affairs.

GENERAL LAW ORGANIZATION

California cities may now be organized through either general state law or individual local charters. Complying with a state constitutional mandate, the legislature in 1883 adopted the Municipal Corporations Act outlining the general law provisions for city organization.[2] The amended sections of this act, now incorporated in the *Government Code*, provide the basic governmental organization and grant of power for the two remaining classes of California cities. All cities now operating under the general law, with the exception of the fifth-class cities of Santa Ana and Woodland, are sixth-class cities. Thus, "sixth-class city" and "general law city" are virtually synonymous. All other cities function under their own locally framed charters or under special charters, and the provisions of this act are of no importance to them.

Of the state's 304 active cities, 242 are operating under these general law provisions.[3] Slightly more than 1,500,000 Californians live in such cities. These cities constitute about 80 per cent of the total number of incorporated areas and contain 22 per cent of the people living within city limits. They range in population from Trinidad in Humboldt County with 94 to South Gate in Los Angeles County with 50,674. Their populations average 6,200.

A sixth-class city has five major characteristics.[4] One, it possesses the usual attributes of a municipal corporation in that it may sue and be sued, has perpetual succession, and may purchase, lease, and hold real and personal property. Two, its government is vested in a five-member council, a clerk, treasurer, chief of police, judge, and others for which later provision can be made. The councilmen, serv-

---

[2] *Cal. Stats.* 1883, p. 93.

[3] The incorporated towns of Hornitos (Mariposa County), Linden (San Joaquin), Markleeville (Alpine), and Meadowlake (Nevada), which are inactive, are not included in this count. General law cities that have incorporated since 1945 are: Barstow (San Bernardino County), Brentwood (Contra Costa), Capitola (Santa Cruz), Coachella (Riverside), Folsom (Sacramento), Galt (Sacramento), Gonzales (Monterey), Greenfield (Monterey), Guadalupe (Santa Barbara), Kerman (Fresno), Live Oak (Sutter), Millbrae (San Mateo), Orange Cove (Fresno), Pismo Beach (San Luis Obispo), Port Hueneme (Ventura), Portola (Plumas), Ripon (San Joaquin), San Pablo (Contra Costa), and Wasco (Kern).

[4] League of California Cities, *Compilation of Laws Relating to Cities of the Sixth Class* (rev. ed., 1947).

City Organization and Governmental Forms

ing four-year terms, must be elected. The clerk and treasurer are also elected in most sixth-class cities, but they may be appointed by the council if the voters approve such an arrangement. The chief of police, judge, and other officers are appointed by the council. Three, either the council-manager or mayor-council form of government may be adopted. Four, council members receive no compensation unless this is approved by the voters, who may increase or decrease the amount at a subsequent election. The council determines the salaries of the clerk, treasurer, and of all other officers and employees. Five, a broad grant of power and authority is conferred upon the city council.

In addition to the inclusive grant of authority "to pass ordinances not in conflict with the constitution and laws of this state or of the United States," a city council of a sixth-class city possesses thirty-two other enumerated powers. These include the right to:

(a) Contract for water supply, and purchase waterworks.

(b) Build and improve bridges, parks, and streets, and make other improvements.

(c) Construct and maintain drains and sewers.

(d) Provide fire protection.

(e) Exercise various financial powers regarding taxes, licenses, and franchises. Without majority approval of the voters, the property tax, excluding money needed for pension plans, flood protection, and certain other activities, must not exceed one dollar on each hundred dollars of property valuation.

(f) Improve rivers and waters.

(g) Acquire, own, construct, maintain, and operate numerous public utilities, including bus lines, street railways, steam railway spur tracks, telephone and telegraph lines, gas and other works for light, power, and heat, public libraries, museums, gymnasiums, parks, and baths. Grant franchises for construction of such public utilities as it deems proper.

(h) Impose fines up to $500 and fix penalties up to six months of imprisonment for violations of city ordinances.

(i) Regulate building construction and repair and building materials.

(j) Regulate signs and advertising.

(k) Issue subpoenas for the attendance of witnesses, or the production of books or other documents, for the purpose of producing evidence or testimony in actions or proceedings pending before the city council.

(l) Expend monies (not exceeding 5 per cent of the total accruing to the general fund in any fiscal year) for music and promotion.

(m) Provide pension or retirement system for city employees, or contract for such service with the state employees' retirement system.

(n) Contract with private individuals or agencies for special services.

(o) Establish and maintain a municipal hospital after popular petition and majority vote.

(p) Contract with a neighboring municipality, the county, or a county fire or police protection district for the furnishing of supplementary fire or police protection.

(q) Enter into agreements with the national government regarding the acquisition, maintenance, and operation of its water system and the sale and distribution of its water.

(r) Acquire property for public purposes.

(s) Provide for a chief executive who during periods of great public calamity will have complete authority over the city and exercise all police power vested in the city by the laws and constitution of California.

The several major advantages generally claimed for cities operating under the general state law as sixth-class cities may be stated in six propositions. 1. California has a modern and well developed series of laws, collectively known as the Municipal Corporations Act. It sets down broad principles covering many municipal functions and leaves adequate discretion to local citizens and their public officials. It also enables a city to choose between the mayor-council and city manager forms of local government. 2. Since provisions of the Municipal Corporations Act are extensive enough to take care of the problems of most medium-sized cities, a city does not need a local charter unless it has some special or peculiar local problem. 3. There is very little likelihood that the state legislature will add damaging amendments to or emasculate the Municipal Corporations Act. Acting through their League of California Cities, municipalities are vigilant and effective in protecting the provisions of the Act. They are responsible for its present modern and adequate status. 4. It is easier for a special interest group to secure amendment of a city's freeholder charter than it is to secure change in the state legislation. There is thus more possibility that such a group might add damaging sections to the freeholder charter. 5. In drafting local charters, boards of freeholders sometimes use new terminology and ambiguous phrases instead of adopting words which have been subject to judicial interpretation. As a consequence, it is possible that legal difficulties will arise in determining the exact meaning and intent of certain sections of a freeholder charter. 6. The $1.00 tax

City Organization and Governmental Forms 17

limit imposed upon cities of the sixth class may be increased by a majority of the voters of such cities.[5]

FREEHOLDER CHARTER ORGANIZATION

Sixty or about one-fifth of the cities in California are operating under locally determined charters. Slightly more than 5,600,000 people live in charter cities, or approximately 80 per cent of the total population living within city limits. They range in population from Grass Valley in Nevada County with 5,242 to Los Angeles with 1,957,692. Their average population, including Los Angeles which has about one-third of their total, is 93,470. Los Angeles excluded, the average drops to 61,939.

Any California city containing more than 3,500 people may adopt its own charter by following the procedure set forth in the state constitution.[6] This process is initiated through an election upon the question of drafting a charter and to choose a board of fifteen freeholders. The election may be called either by a two-thirds vote of the city council or by a petition signed by 15 per cent of the qualified electors of the city. If a majority of the voters favor drafting a charter, the fifteen freeholder candidates receiving the greatest number of votes at the same election are given the responsibility of drafting a charter within a period of one year. An optional method is to have a charter framed by the city council or its representatives.

A majority vote in favor of the charter is required for local ratification. The charter is then submitted to the state legislature at its next session where it must receive a majority vote in both houses. No charter has yet failed to get legislative ratification. After local sanction and state legislative approval, the charter is filed with the secretary of state. Charter amendments may be proposed by the city council or by a petition containing signatures of 15 per cent of the city voters. They also must be approved by a majority of the city voters and by the state legislature.

Freeholder charters illustrate the doctrine of home rule for cities. Briefly stated, it is the power given to cities by state constitutional provisions to frame and adopt their own charters, and to have supremacy in municipal affairs. The reasoning behind the doctrine of municipal home rule is that each city is a natural social and economic unit having its individual problems of self-government. It is held that therefore citizens of individual cities are in a better posi-

---

[5] *Cal. Stats.* 1947, chap. 1343, changed the voting requirement from two-thirds to a majority.
[6] *Cal. Const.*, Art. XI, sec. 8.

tion than the state legislature to decide what organization and functions they need. It should be noted also that recent developments in general state law affecting sixth-class cities have similarly been directed toward these objectives by providing for optional forms of government and for a rather broad grant of power.

TABLE 1

California Local Charter Cities

City	Population 1950 preliminary census	Date of first and present charter	City	Population 1950 preliminary census	Date of first and present charter
Alameda	62,242	1907, 1937	Pomona	35,160	1911
Albany	17,545	1927	Porterville	6,857	1927
Alhambra	51,225	1915	Redondo Beach	25,176	1935, 1949
Bakersfield	34,540	1915	Redwood City	25,342	1929
Berkeley	112,125	1895, 1909	Richmond	99,163	1909
Burbank	78,224	1927	Riverside	46,399	1907, 1929
Chico	12,210	1923	Roseville	8,685	1935
Chula Vista	15,844	1949	Sacramento	134,313	1893, 1921
Compton	47,893	1925	Salinas	13,892	1903, 1919
Culver City	19,560	1947	San Bernardino	62,694	1905
Eureka	22,926	1895	San Diego	321,485	1889, 1931
Fresno	90,626	1901, 1921	San Francisco	760,381	1898, 1931
Glendale	94,993	1921	San Jose	95,020	1897, 1915
Grass Valley	5,242	1893, 1921	San Leandro	27,485	1933, 1949
Huntington Beach	5,258	1937	San Luis Obispo	14,162	1911
Inglewood	45,942	1927	San Mateo	41,531	1923
Long Beach	243,921	1907, 1921	San Rafael	13,830	1913
Los Angeles	1,957,692	1889, 1925	Santa Barbara	44,759	1899, 1927
Marysville	7,777	1919	Santa Clara	11,668	1927
Merced	15,001	1949	Santa Cruz	21,848	1907, 1948
Modesto	17,319	1911	Santa Monica	70,843	1907, 1947
Monterey	16,120	1911, 1925	Santa Rosa	17,905	1903, 1923
Napa	13,542	1893, 1915	Stockton	71,276	1889, 1923
Oakland	382,463	1889, 1911	Sunnyvale	9,849	1949
Oroville	5,345	1933	Torrance	22,201	1947
Pacific Grove	9,573	1927	Tulare	12,367	1923
Palo Alto	25,290	1909	Vallejo	23,164	1899, 1946
Pasadena	103,971	1901	Ventura	16,532	1931, 1933
Petaluma	10,390	1911, 1947	Visalia	11,670	1923
Piedmont	10,121	1923	Watsonville	11,516	1903

The entire subject of freeholder charters including the doctrine of municipal home rule has received voluminous interpretations by the state courts of California. From these numerous and sometimes conflicting decisions, several fairly well settled principles can be deduced. First, a freeholder charter when ratified by the state legis-

City Organization and Governmental Forms

lature becomes a law of the legislature. It automatically repeals any inconsistent general statutes dealing with municipal affairs of the city. Second, a chartered city is independent of general state laws dealing with municipal affairs and its charter prevails over the general law wherever there is a conflict. It is advisable however, that the charter have a blanket clause giving the city power over "all municipal affairs except as limited by the charter." General state laws operate within chartered cities in matters of state policy.

Third, the important question of "what is a municipal affair?" must be left to judicial interpretation. There has never been a clear court definition of "municipal affairs" in California. This has necessitated separate court decisions as questions have arisen concerning specific municipal activities. It is a slow process of judicial inclusion and exclusion. Some matters are thus municipal affairs: compensation and pensions of city employees; election and removal of municipal officers; provision for certain public utilities; prosecutions for violations of the city charter and municipal ordinances; opening, widening, and maintenance of streets; bridge construction and repair; and regulation of charges of a public service corporation within city limits. Others have been determined to be state affairs and not under the jurisdiction of charter cities: organization and control of school districts; disposition of fines for misdemeanors in violation of state laws; organization, consolidation, and annexation of territory; and streets declared to be secondary highways.

There are several major benefits generally accruing to a city through adoption of a freeholder charter. A freeholder charter gives the people of the community an opportunity to have the kind of government they themselves want, both as to form of organization and functions to be exercised. Preparing a freeholder charter creates public interest in civic affairs because it places the responsibility for community development directly in the hands of the citizens of the city. It is often easier to revise and amend a freeholder charter locally than it is to have the state legislature change the Municipal Corporations Act. On the other hand, the city is not subject to the whim of the state legislature in municipal affairs should the legislature make some undesirable change in the Municipal Corporations Act. Local government tends to be more adaptable to local conditions and needs under a freeholder charter than it is under the system of uniform state legislation. A charter city has extremely broad authority to develop new tax sources, unless limited by its own charter provisions, whereas a general law city has only those taxing powers specifically conferred upon it by statute. A charter city may set its own tax rate limitation. It may leave the property tax rate at $1.00

per $100 assessed valuation as it is under the Municipal Corporations Act, or it may extend the rate beyond this limitation or choose to set none at all. This factor has influenced some large cities, that required additional revenue from property taxation, to adopt charters.

Many charters are too technical and too long. Their provisions can generally be classified according to (1) the powers of the city, including corporate, proprietary, and governmental powers, (2) organizational provisions covering the local legislature or council, executive and administrative organization (including the mayor or city manager, department heads, and boards), essential principles of organization within departments and bureaus, and organizational relationships, (3) certain basic procedures or safeguards for such activities as nominations and elections, council and board proceedings, granting of franchises, and tax assessment and collection, (4) modern administrative practices such as the merit system, and budget and central financial management and accounting, and (5) popular controls over the government.[7] Most details should be omitted from charters and those which are essential should be incorporated into an administrative code. It is most important that the charter be concise, clear, consistent, flexible, and responsive to the people.

One hundred and sixty-five California cities contain the minimum population required to draft their own charters. The main reasons for the failure of about two-thirds of them to use this privilege are satisfaction with the general state laws applicable to non-charter cities and/or local inertia. There is an apparent tendency for cities to prepare and adopt charters before their areas have become heavily populated. All five which have adopted charters since 1947—Chula Vista, Culver City, Merced, Sunnyvale, and Torrance—had fewer than 20,000 inhabitants at the time of adoption. All cities of more than 30,000 except two—Santa Ana and South Gate—operate under home-rule charters. Most of the eligible cities that do not possess charters have less than 10,000 people.

Who initiated the charter? What has been done in the past? What is the ability of the city to finance improved municipal services? What is the degree of interest and support for the new charter from community civic organizations? Answers to these types of questions greatly affect the success or failure of individual charters.[8]

---

[7] National Municipal League, *A Guide for Charter Commissions* (1947), pp. 18–19. This manual should be used in connection with another League publication, *Model City Charter*, the latest edition of which was published in 1941. Another valuable aid is Thomas H. Reed's *Revising a City Charter* (1947), issued by the Governmental Research Association in New York.

[8] *Western City*, Vol. 23 (March, 1947), 38.

City Organization and Governmental Forms

MAYOR-COUNCIL FORM

The mayor-council system, oldest of the three principal forms of city government in California, consists of an executive or presiding officer (the mayor); a legislative body (the council) of five to fifteen members, elected at large or from wards and responsible for enacting local laws; and varying numbers of elected or appointed department heads and administrative boards. California mayors are either elected by the voters or elevated to the position by a vote of the elected council from among its own membership. However, striking variations exist within the mayor-council plan. The distinctions are largely determined not by quality of personnel but through relationships existing between mayor and council.

In all general law cities and many charter cities in California, the mayor is simply the presiding officer of the council. Except to the extent that these cities have conferred it upon a city manager, all final administrative authority rests with the council as a whole, not with the mayor. The latter is chosen from among the council membership by its majority vote. In such instances, the mayor has no exclusive powers of appointing administrative personnel nor does he have authority to veto acts of the council. All of these cities belong to one variation of the mayor-council form. In addition, some charter cities which provide for the election by the people of the mayor, independent of the council, belong to this first variety of mayor-council city in which the mayor has only limited powers. They generally require confirmation by the council of the mayor's appointments to administrative positions, and prohibit the mayor from vetoing acts of the council. On the other hand, a few of the California charter cities concentrate substantial administrative and legislative responsibilities in the mayor, and therefore constitute a second major variation of mayor-council organization. Individual mayors may, in addition, through political position and personal prestige, influence the relationship of their offices to the city council and to other parts of the city government. There is no assurance of continuous administrative leadership under any of these variations. The mayor-council system is still the most prevalent form of city government in California and in the nation generally.

COMMISSION FORM

In the commission form of urban local government five commissioners are elected by popular vote. They serve as the legislature of the city, and in addition, each of them directs an administrative department. Sacramento was the first commission city in the United States, adopting the form in 1863.[9] The main feature of the system as it functioned in Sacramento was the election of three trustees who simultaneously served together as the city's legislative body, and separately as directors of the police, fire, and water departments. A mayor and council replaced the commission system in 1893.

After the plan was revived and popularized nationally through its adoption by Galveston, Texas, and Des Moines, Iowa, in the early years of the twentieth century, numerous cities in California and elsewhere experimented with the system. The idea expanded until 1917 when more than five hundred cities in the United States were governed by commissions. A reverse trend then got under way, and during the last thirty-three years there has been a steady decline, and very few adoptions. Since Vallejo and Santa Monica abandoned the system in 1947 in favor of the council-manager form, Fresno is the only charter city in California operating as a commission city.[10]

Although their major officers are mayors and councilmen, many less populous general law cities in California are functioning under a modified commission plan. In such instances, the five councilmen, generally at their initial meeting after the local election, decide which of them shall be mayor and specify what city functions, usually public works, finance, and police and fire, shall become the special interest of individual council members. Councilmen in sixth-class cities have absolutely no power except when acting at a meeting of the city council. As a legislative body, they have powers conferred upon them by law. As individual councilmen, they have no authority. They are not department heads and any purported exercise of administrative authority is illegally assumed and is wholly without a statutory basis. Since 1947, sixth-class cities (which include all general law cities with only two exceptions) can use either the mayor-council or council-manager form of government, but are unable to adopt the commission system.

Because their mayors and councilmen act as part-time departmental *advisors* rather than full-time administrators, many small California cities will in practice probably continue to use the modified commission form. However, many cities that have abandoned the plan did so because of a common, serious defect—diffu-

---

[9] *Cal. Stats.* 1863, p. 415.

[10] Section 6 of the Fresno city charter states that "Except as otherwise expressly provided in this charter, the legislative power of the city and general administrative control of the city government . . . shall be vested in a City Commission . . . composed of the Commissioner of Public Safety and Welfare and ex officio Mayor, the Commissioner of Finance, the Commissioner of Public Works, and two . . . Legislative Commissioners."

sion of administrative responsibility among five commissioners. The absence of a single, unifying executive usually meant little coördination of city activities, much duplication of effort, and frequent friction between department heads who were not elected upon the basis of their qualifications to be directors of city administrative departments. Cities in California have been turning away from the commission form in favor of the council-manager and mayor-council systems.

COUNCIL-MANAGER FORM

The council-manager form of city government, frequently termed the chief contribution of the United States to municipal administration, contains several major identifying features. The elected city council determines all municipal policies not set forth in the city charter or the state general laws, enacts local ordinances, votes appropriations, and appoints and may remove a chief administrator, the city manager. Neither the mayor, who is usually appointed by the council from among its own members, nor the council interferes with the administrative functions of the manager. The council deals with administration only through the city manager, and these administrative functions are never delegated to council committees or members.

Another important requirement of the council-manager plan is that the city manager's authority be commensurate with his responsibilities as head of the city's administration. There is general agreement among students of municipal government that he should have most, or all, of the following duties: (1) to see that all laws and ordinances are enforced; (2) to exercise control over all departments and in accordance with civil service regulations appoint, supervise, and remove department heads and subordinate employees of the city; (3) to make such recommendations to the council concerning the affairs of the city as may seem to him desirable; (4) to keep the council advised of the financial condition and future needs of the city; (5) to prepare and submit to the council the annual budget; (6) to prepare and submit such reports as may be required by that body; (7) to keep the public informed, through reports to the council, regarding the operations of the city government; and (8) to perform such other duties as may be prescribed by charter, state law, or council ordinance or resolution.[11]

California city managers generally possess all the foregoing elements of authority. The major management functions usually vested

---

[11] International City Managers' Association, *Recent Council-Manager Developments and Directory of Council-Manager Cities* (April, 1950), p. 4.

in them are, in order of frequency: preparation of budget for current operations; conduct of administrative planning; preparation of budget for capital improvements; control of expenditures; coördination and direction of operations; appointment and removal of personnel; and representation of the city in discussions of administrative and policy questions concerning intergovernmental relations.[12]

Through appointment of city managers or chief administrative officers, one hundred or almost one-third of all cities in California have centralized part or all of their administrative management in one person. Sixty-seven of these one hundred cities, or almost 70 per cent, are approved as council-manager cities by the International City Managers' Association. This sanction is based not upon the professional qualifications of individual management officials, but upon the degree of responsibility given to them by city councils. The major reason why many of the thirty-three cities operating under some form of centralized professional administration did not adopt the full council-manager plan as defined by the International City Managers' Association is found in the state legislation existing before 1947. Before 1947, the office of city manager could be created in general law cities only by vote of the people. The council of a general law city could, however, enact an ordinance providing for a chief administrative officer whose powers were limited to making budget, personnel, and purchasing recommendations, subject to councilmanic ratification, and to coördinating departmental activities. Such an officer does not possess the direct administrative authority given to city managers operating in approved council-manager cities. In practice, however, he may be able to operate virtually as a city manager so long as the council supports his decisions. Since 1947 it has been possible for general law city councils to enact ordinances establishing the full council-manager form of government, and a limited number of general law cities have already taken advantage of this opportunity to change over from a chief administrative officer to a manager.[13]

Even excluding the thirty-three cities which have partly centralized their professional management, 24 per cent or almost one of every four California cities having at least 1,000 people is a council-manager city. This is more than twice the national average of 11.3

---

[12] Richard Graves, "Council-Manager Government in California Cities," *Western City*, Vol. 23 (June, 1947), 28. Early council-manager developments are recounted in R. M. Dorton's "The City Manager Plan in California" (unpublished M.A. thesis, University of California, Berkeley, 1925).

[13] *Cal. Stats.* 1947, chap. 614.

TABLE 2

California Charter and General Law Cities Appointing City Managers or Chief Administrative Officers

Charter cities	Population (1950 preliminary census data)	General law cities	Population (1950 preliminary census data)
Alameda*	62,242	Antioch*	10,973
Alhambra*	51,225	Auburn*	4,577
Bakersfield*	34,540	Avalon	1,490
Berkeley*	112,125	Claremont*	6,216
Burbank*	78,224	Corona	10,219
Chico*	12,210	Coronado*	12,423
Chula Vista*	15,844	Daly City	15,066
Compton*	47,893	Davis	3,557
Culver City	19,560	Delano*	8,672
Glendale*	94,993	Dixon	1,710
Huntington Beach	5,173	El Cajon	5,418
Inglewood	45,942	El Cerrito*	18,015
Long Beach*	243,921	El Monte	8,073
Merced*	15,001	El Segundo	8,008
Monterey*	16,120	Escondido	6,608
Napa*	13,542	Fillmore*	3,879
Oakland*	382,463	Glendora	3,954
Oroville	5,345	Hanford	9,829
Pacific Grove*	9,573	Hawthorne*	16,267
Palo Alto	25,920	Hayward*	14,246
Pasadena*	103,971	Hemet*	3,371
Petaluma*	10,390	Hillsborough*	3,512
Pomona	31,329	Lincoln	2,404
Porterville*	6,857	Lindsay	5,033
Redondo Beach*	25,176	Lodi*	14,370
Redwood City*	25,342	Lynwood*	25,534
Richmond*	99,163	Manhattan Beach*	17,243
Sacramento*	134,313	Martinez	8,215
Salinas*	13,892	Menlo Park*	13,537
San Bernardino	62,694	Mill Valley*	7,241
San Diego*	321,485	Monrovia*	20,015
San Francisco	760,381	Montebello	21,754
San Jose*	95,020	Monterey Park*	20,102
San Leandro*	27,485	National City	21,123
San Mateo*	41,531	Newport Beach*	12,220

TABLE 2 (continued)

California Charter and General Law Cities Appointing City Managers or Chief Administrative Officers

Charter cities	Population (1950 preliminary census data)	General law cities	Population (1950 preliminary census data)
San Rafael	13,830	North Sacramento	6,016
Santa Cruz*	21,848	Oceanside	12,880
Santa Monica*	70,843	Ontario*	22,820
Santa Rosa*	17,905	Oxnard*	21,512
Stockton*	71,276	Palm Springs*	7,428
Sunnyvale*	9,849	Pittsburg*	12,662
Torrance*	22,201	Redding*	10,136
Tulare*	12,367	Redlands*	18,407
Vallejo*	23,164	San Carlos*	14,339
Ventura*	16,532	San Gabriel	20,205
Visalia*	11,670	San Marino	11,198
		Santa Paula	11,034
		South Pasadena*	16,925
		South San Francisco*	19,250
		Turlock	6,221
		Ukiah	6,134
		Upland*	9,125
		West Covina	4,511
		Woodland*	9,318

* These cities are in the International City Managers' Association directory of approved council-manager cities (International City Managers' Association, *Recent Council-Manager Developments and Directory of Council-Manager Cities* (1950), pp. 11-12). Gilroy (4,953), which has a chief administrative officer and is not in the directory, is omitted from this table because it operates under a special legislative charter.

per cent. Furthermore, approved council-manager cities in California surpass the national average in all population classifications except those of 1,000 to 2,500 and 2,500 to 5,000. These variations are most pronounced among the larger cities. The number of California cities of 50,000 to 100,000 population with recognized council-manager governments is more than double the national average. In addition, seven of the nine California cities possessing more than 100,000 inhabitants in 1949—Berkeley, Long Beach, Oakland, Pasadena, Richmond, Sacramento, and San Diego—have accredited council-manager governments. This is 77 per cent or more than three times the national average of 24 per cent. More than 2,840,000 people or about 40 per cent of the population now residing within California cities live in these sixty-seven approved council-manager cities. More than 3,940,000 residents or more than 55 per cent of the city dwellers in the state are governed by the one hundred cities having complete or partial professional administrative management.

TABLE 3

California and U. S. Council-Manager Cities of More than 1,000 Population, December, 1949

Population	Number of active California cities	Number of California council-manager cities approved by International City Managers' Association	Per cent of California cities having approved council-manager government	Per cent of cities in United States having approved council-manager government
1,000–2,500	73	0	0	3.4
2,500–5,000	57	4	7.0	11.3
5,000–10,000	50	11	22.0	20.4
10,000–25,000	63	32	50.8	26.3
25,000–50,000	14	6	42.9	28.3
50,000–100,000	9	7	77.8	32.0
Over 100,000	9	7	77.8	23.9
Total	275	67	24.4	11.3

Nationally, among states which are similar in not having townships or New England type towns as a significant part of their local governmental systems, California ranks second proportionately in number of approved council-manager cities. The leader is Virginia where fifty or 24 per cent of the cities have managers. This exceeds California's 22 per cent based on sixty-seven of three hundred and four cities. Florida has 18.9 per cent. The seventy-seven council-manager cities in Texas, the fourth ranking state, represent only 11.8 per cent of the total incorporated places.

The trend toward council-manager government is easily the most significant recent development in California city government. It is being fostered by the intensification and multiplication of problems confronting councilmen in rapidly growing cities. These local legislators, particularly those in general law cities who can be expected to devote only a limited portion of their time to public business, feel compelled to delegate administrative planning and duties to a professional administrator hired by and directly accountable to them. It is then the manager's responsibility to unify the personnel and departmental programs and policies in order that the various parts of the city government may work harmoniously toward accomplishing the program determined by the council.

The three methods of instituting the council-manager plan in California have all been used. They are: (1) inclusion in the locally drawn charter (for example, Long Beach, Oakland, San Diego); (2) adoption through ordinance approved by majority vote of the council (Auburn, Richmond, South Pasadena); and (3) ratification, by majority vote of the local residents, of an ordinance submitted by a council majority (Hillsborough, Palm Springs, Redding). The first and third methods are available to charter and general law cities respectively.[14] Both types of cities may use the second method. When the council-manager system is based on a charter provision or an ordinance approved by popular vote after referral by the council, a subsequent vote of the people is required to abolish the office of the city manager. Of course this in no way affects the council's power of appointment and removal of a specific manager, a power basic to the system itself. The plan is much more susceptible to abandonment because of irrelevant or hasty action when it is founded solely on a council ordinance, repealable at any time by a simple majority vote of the city council. Several California cities have abolished the manager plan by rescinding their manager ordinances, but only Santa Barbara has abandoned this governmental form by a referendum vote of the people (1927).

---

[14] Details relating to the various methods of adopting the council-manager plan, and provisions limiting its application, are contained in *Deering's General Laws*, Act 5233.

CHAPTER III

City Functions and Finance

The functions of city government are to provide almost all the publicly supported services which distinguish an urban from a rural environment. They are grouped under the headings of general government, protection to persons and property, public works, public service enterprises, charities and corrections, health, education, and recreation. The auxiliary and regulative activities are largely contained in the general government grouping; the service functions under the remaining headings.

GENERAL GOVERNMENT

General government in municipalities includes the legislative and executive functions, financial activities, judicial duties, elections, and important work related to the executive and legislative functions such as purchasing, personnel, management of other common services, and planning. Expenditures for these activities totaled $33,577,000 in 1949, 11.5 per cent of all city costs.[1]

Legislative and Executive Functions.—The city councils have final responsibility for all municipal governmental activity. Theirs is primarily a legislative function involving policy determination, ordinance enactment, tax rate establishment, and budget approval. The city councils' control over the municipal government is more clearly defined than is that of the average county board of supervisors because of the absence or smaller number of independently elected officials.

The major executive functions are appointment of officers and employees, day-to-day supervision of activities, preparation of the budget, and control of fiscal affairs. The precise location of these duties is not always well defined. Although the gradual separation of

---
[1] Financial data contained in this chapter are obtained primarily from: State Controller, *Annual Report of Financial Transactions of Municipalities and Counties of California for the Fiscal Year Ending June 30, 1949* (1950). (Hereafter cited as *Annual Report of Financial Transactions.*) San Francisco finances have been excluded because of that city's partial resemblance to a county.

executive functions from the legislative body has moved further in cities than it has in counties, there is still a blurring of boundaries. Particularly in general law cities executive duties may rest largely with the council. In these cities the city clerk does much work of an executive nature and fills an office second in importance only to the legislative body itself. Another complicating factor is the frequent existence of park, recreation, library, harbor, and other commissions which may exercise executive authority over important segments of the city's government. In the council-manager city, however, and in the mayor-council city when the mayor has well-defined authority (as in some charter cities), the separation of powers is generally evident, and the executive function is vested primarily in the manager or mayor.[2]

Fiscal Operations.—Control of the two fundamental fiscal operations of budget-making and tax-levying is the province of the legislative body. The other fiscal duties—assessment and collection of taxes, maintenance of the treasury, preparation of the budget, and conduct of an audit—are variously handled.

Cities may either do their own assessing and collecting of property taxes, or they may contract with the counties to perform these services. Approximately one-half the cities follow the latter procedure. Collection of taxes and licenses, when done by the city, is handled either by the tax collector or by the clerk, frequently the latter. The chief of police serves as ex officio tax collector in general law cities, unless the ordinance provides otherwise.

The broad functions of the treasurer are receipt and payment of public funds, together with maintenance of adequate protection against possible losses on the part of depositories with whom public funds may be placed. Budget preparation, a crucial operation in the administrative process, is the responsibility of the manager in council-manager cities. In the others, unless a strong mayor's office has taken over the function, budget preparation is carried out by the individual city departments, the city clerk, and the council.

The administrative preaudit is, in a few cities, the work of an officer appointed by the city manager, and in some other cities of an officer appointed by the mayor or council. In general law cities either the auditor or the city clerk performs this function. The postaudit may be handled by the auditor, the clerk, or by an independent firm of accountants.

---

[2] The broad problems of municipal organization and management, as well as the more detailed questions of operating procedure, are receiving close scrutiny by such groups as the League of California Cities, Public Administration Service, Louis J. Kroeger and Associates, and others.

City Functions and Finance

Administration of Justice.—Until the passage and implementation of a 1950 constitutional amendment providing for reorganization of the inferior courts, those courts most closely related to municipal government were of varied jurisdiction and designation. Among them were municipal courts, police courts, city courts, and city justices' courts. They generally exercised concurrent jurisdiction with the township justices of the peace in both civil and criminal actions, but their jurisdictions were in most instances restricted to actions arising within the corporate limits of the city. A few were given some extended jurisdiction within their counties. Except for the municipal courts[3] they did not have exclusive jurisdiction within the city but shared it with the township justice. All these courts were primarily concerned with violations of city ordinances or any matter in which the city was a party or in which it might be interested. The procedure and manner of appeal corresponded to that of a justice's court.

The recent constitutional amendment greatly simplified and clarified inferior court structure. It provided for only two types of inferior courts, municipal courts and justice courts. The type of court to be established in any area depends upon the population. The amendment called for division of the state into districts by the legislature. Those districts having a population of more than 40,000 are to be served by a municipal court; those having a smaller population by a justice court; no district can have more than one inferior court. Judges in both kinds of courts are elective. The passage of this amendment is an important step toward reduction in the number and variety of inferior courts and solves completely the troublesome problem of overlapping jurisdictions. It will undoubtedly facilitate the work of the judicial council in coördinating and directing the work of the courts.

Municipal law officers, usually called city attorneys, have a wide range of duties in addition to prosecuting violations of state laws or city ordinances. They serve as legal advisors to the councils, draft ordinances, prepare legal documents for the cities, and represent them in civil cases. Thus important functions of guidance for the city council are performed by the city attorney, particularly in legal matters and in policy matters touching on legal questions. These officers are appointed by the council in sixth-class cities and in most charter cities.

Electoral System.—Municipal election procedure operates for those municipal elections which have not been consolidated with

---

[3] Municipal courts could be established in chartered cities of more than 40,000 population and were found in seven of California's larger cities.

a county, state or national election. The city council appoints an inspector, a judge, and clerks as election officials for each precinct. The city clerk assumes those election duties fulfilled by the county clerk in county and state-wide elections.

Purchasing.—Central purchasing of supplies for the municipality is one of the major housekeeping functions frequently found under the control of the executive. Although it is much more definitely characteristic of larger cities, central purchasing is beginning to spread among the smaller municipalities, and practically all charter and council-manager cities practice some form of centralization. However, decentralized purchasing still characterizes a large proportion of the sixth-class cities.

The achievement of greater economy in city operations is the primary aim of centralized purchasing. Under such an arrangement little direct purchasing by the individual departments is allowed. Instead, they requisition needed goods and services, which are then supplied on the most economical basis by the purchasing agent. In larger cities the duties of the purchasing agent demand a full-time officer, but in smaller cities the function may be performed by some other city official on a part-time basis. Thus city managers, clerks, councilmen, and engineers sometimes serve in the capacity of purchasing agents.

Personnel.—Under the general law any city can adopt a personnel or civil service system which may vary in elaborateness from simple minimum standards of qualification and employment to a comprehensive formal civil service plan. The chief elements of an adequate personnel or civil service system are (1) a job classification plan and salary schedule, (2) an established method of recruitment and promotion, the former, at least, being based on competitive examination, and (3) a personnel officer to administer the system. In addition an independent personnel board with well-defined powers may be necessary to protect tenure in those cities where politics has traditionally influenced recruitment.[4] There is danger, however, that a personnel commission with power to set aside orders, particularly dismissals, of the city administration may become a hindrance to effective management.[5] In cities with a history of efficient government a less formal system closely tied to the executive authority should be quite satisfactory.

There is wide civil service coverage of municipal personnel in

---

[4] "Personnel Administration," *Western City*, Vol. 26 (June, 1950), 47.
[5] Public Administration Service, *The City Government of Oakland, California* (1948), pp. 92–93.

City Functions and Finance

California cities of more than 25,000 population.[6] Three-fourths of these cities report that all their employees come under civil service and only 13 per cent specify that none is under civil service. Both these figures indicate a significantly higher coverage than the nationwide average. Among the smaller cities, 10,000 to 25,000, civil service is much less comprehensive than in the larger, but nevertheless they are well above the mass of American cities in this respect. Approximately one-half of California's cities in this group report coverage for all their personnel, and only about one-third report *no coverage.*

Among cities in both population groups the civil service systems are most frequently supervised by a board appointed by the council or mayor, although in the larger cities the personnel officer may perform this function, and in smaller cities the manager may do so. Direct personnel administration in those cities having boards is usually performed by a full-time appointive officer in the larger cities and by the manager in the smaller cities. In some instances the city clerk, the manager's assistant, individual department heads, or other officers may handle personnel matters.

Because of the expense of carrying on certain centralized personnel operations, the possibility of coöperative action by two or more jurisdictions has been investigated. Smaller communities in particular are finding it advantageous to contract with other agencies or with outside private groups for the establishment of a personnel classification system, and for recruitment and testing. This kind of development is most widely used in the Los Angeles area where the county, cities, and school districts coöperate on various bases.[7] Many of the cities contract with the county for personnel services while others contract with the State Personnel Board. Special coöperative arrangements have been worked out between the City of Los Angeles, the County of Los Angeles, and the Los Angeles City Schools.

Cities may provide employee retirement benefits in any of several ways. They may establish their own systems, arrange for inclusion of firemen and policemen in the county peace officers and fire service retirement plans, or contract with the State Employees' Retirement System to cover any or all city personnel. Larger cities in most cases maintain their own plans, while the smaller cities

---

[6] International City Managers' Association, *The Municipal Yearbook, 1950* (1950), pp. 146–173. Care should be exercised in interpreting these population groupings as they are based on 1940 census data.

[7] Judith N. Jamison, *Intergovernmental Coöperation in Public Personnel Administration in the Los Angeles Area,* University of California, Los Angeles, Bureau of Governmental Research (1944), pp. 1–9.

generally contract with the state system. The proportion of cities with full employee coverage is approximately the same for both population groups, 60 per cent in each instance reporting inclusion of all employees. However, whereas no larger city reports that none of its employees is covered, one fourth of the smaller cities so indicate.

Management of Other Common Services.—The central management of a number of common services in addition to purchasing and personnel is receiving attention even in some of the smaller cities. Common office services, building management, printing and duplicating, transportation, and equipment are frequently provided by a regular department or a special agency. In some smaller cities the clerk's office may handle the messenger service, printing and duplicating, and building management; or the public works department may be responsible for building management, and the purchasing agent may provide printing and duplicating service. In the largest cities a department of administrative management may supply many of these common services.[8]

The office services which may be centralized include mailing, messenger service, tabulating, and telephone service. Building management covers the allocation of office space to various departments, supervision of janitorial services, and planning of major maintenance and repair work. Transportation and equipment services usually mean maintenance of a central garage and a fleet of motor vehicles. These are services which must be provided in all municipalities either centrally, or on a department-by-department basis. Advantages of central management that even the smaller cities can obtain include lower unit costs, specialized supervision, and better handling of peak work-loads.

Planning.—A number of factors are operating to force the realization by most California cities of the need to plan for their further growth. The rapid population increase in urban areas, wartime and postwar population shifts, and intensified housing, traffic and transit problems, have combined to emphasize the need for an orderly development that takes future as well as present needs into consideration. The nationwide urban redevelopment program, with its requirement that projects be undertaken as a part of the city's overall plan, is also providing a strong impetus to municipal planning activities. In a few jurisdictions there is a growing awareness of the need for planning that is based on careful study of social and economic factors as well as on purely physical facts.

---

[8] "Management of Common Services," *Public Management*, Vol. 32 (July, 1950), 150–152.

City Functions and Finance

The major aims of municipal planning are summed up in the city's master plan which may include sections on conservation, land use, recreation, streets and highways, transportation, public services and facilities, public buildings, community design, and housing. The master plan acts as a guide for community growth and change and for the studied development of its physical environment to serve economic, social, and cultural needs. Insofar as private development is concerned, the plan is enforced by persuasion and by the use of zoning regulations and subdivision controls. Public phases of the plan are effected through the city's own capital improvements budget, a planning tool of primary importance.

By 1948 about thirty of the more populous cities had made significant planning progress, including work on a land-use plan. A number of others among the one hundred and ninety-three having planning commissions had taken some action. These figures do not, however, reveal the extent to which planning has been made a force in directing the city's growth. Present indications are that a respectable percentage of those cities doing significant planning, particularly the larger ones, are also working to make it effective.

State law permits the creation of planning commissions in any incorporated municipality. In home-rule cities the individual charters provide the framework. In general law cities the commissions may contain from five to nine members who may be persons holding municipal offices, provided that the number who do not hold office exceeds those who do. The commissioners are appointed for four-year terms by the mayor with the consent of the council. The master plan, or sections of it, must be approved by a two-thirds vote of the commission, after which it is presented to the council where a majority vote is sufficient for adoption.

Cities may rely on their own paid staffs to carry on planning activities, or they may retain private consultants. Many of the smaller cities take the latter course when it is not felt that their needs require the work of a full-time planner. Most of the larger cities maintain permanent staffs, but even they frequently call in consultants to assist in specific technical jobs. Cities of more than 50,000 population are likely to employ a full-time planning director, whereas the smaller ones tend to rely on the city manager, the city engineer, or some other official to direct planning activities.

The coördination of planning work among cities within the same region is possible in several ways. County planning commissions may take this responsibility, or regional planning commissions may be established, but the legal requirements involved in organizing those in the latter group place them in a closer relationship with the county planning commissions than with those of the cities. Only one regional planning commission, that in Los Angeles County, has been established. It has, however, assumed major responsibilities for the development of regional plans and for the coördination of activities of other planning agencies operating within the county.[9]

Urban planning commissions, another possible tool of coöperative planning, may be established by resolution of the governing bodies of a city or cities, and/or county or counties in an urban area. Their members are appointed by the chief executive officers of the local governments from their respective planning commissions. No urban planning commissions have been established in California. Other methods of effecting coöperative planning have been evolved to meet specific situations. The East Bay cities, by council resolutions, directed Berkeley to have an area-wide sewage survey made in order that plans for an unified disposal system might be drawn up. Cities in a single region sometimes employ the same private consultant to do their major planning work, thus achieving an informal but effective type of coördination. Coöperative airport planning in the San Francisco Bay area has been realized through the joint efforts of the City of San Francisco, the San Francisco Bay Area Council, and the Bay Area Aviation Committee. Local chambers of commerce and other groups are frequently willing to sponsor or participate in economic, industrial, traffic, or other surveys aiming at improved future development.

Cities may establish zoning restrictions either under the zoning law or as a part of their master plans. Thus certain uses, businesses, and types of structures may be permitted or prohibited in specified areas of the city. In addition a city may be zoned to regulate the shape, size, and general configuration of structures. If a city has a planning commission it must require the commission to recommend the zoning maps and regulations, but in the absence of a commission these are prepared by the council itself. A city may also establish a zoning commission to report on applications for variance permits. The wise use of zoning regulations is an important technique for carrying out the city's master plan.

PROTECTION TO PERSONS AND PROPERTY

Cities protect the persons and property of their citizens through fire and police department activities; maintenance of jails and pounds; building, plumbing, and electrical inspection; and workmen's com-

---

[9] Judith N. Jamison, *Coördinated Public Planning in the Los Angeles Region*, University of California, Los Angeles, Bureau of Governmental Research (1948), p. 73.

City Functions and Finance

pensation and other insurance. Total costs of such protection in 1949 were $94,057,000, almost one-third of all city expenditures. Of this sum slightly more than half was paid out for police activities, one-third for fire departments, and 12 per cent for all other protective work.

Police.—The municipal police force is responsible for the protection of life and property and preservation of the peace. As the chief law enforcement agency of the city the police carry on uniformed patrol activities, traffic regulation, juvenile delinquency control, and detective work. Uniformed patrols are necessary for observation, investigation, suppression of criminal activity, regulation of conduct, and for routine and emergency calls. Although most cities continue to make some use of the policeman on the beat for regular patrol work, they are turning increasingly to the use of radio-equipped automobiles.

Traffic regulation is another important duty of the police, sometimes taking as much as 25 per cent of the total departmental budget. Included in this function are traffic law enforcement, traffic direction, accident investigation, and, frequently, parking meter control. Traffic engineering, a function closely related to planning and public works, is often handled by the police in smaller cities, and in the larger ones by a special traffic engineer who is usually independent of the police department.

The thorough investigation of crimes and suspicious activity that are beyond the scope of the ordinary patrolman constitutes the detective function of police work. Special plain-clothed details are maintained in larger cities to keep constant surveillance over vice, gambling, and narcotic traffic. The immediate aim of detective work is the identification and apprehension of offenders, but the police must also coöperate closely with the district attorney in supplying information for the prosecution of cases.

An adequate program of juvenile control must provide not only for the detection of juvenile delinquency and identification of delinquents, but also for the investigation of conditions underlying such behavior. Remedial measures must then be taken. The most common type of special service relating to juveniles, provided by almost one-half of California cities, is the postoffense supervision of delinquents.[10] Almost one-fifth have a special officer or detail assigned to juveniles. Other police activities relating to juveniles include participation in youth programs and organization of school

---

[10] University of Southern California, School of Public Administration, *Current Practices in Police-Juvenile Relations* (1949), p. 8.

traffic patrols. Although the chief purpose of traffic patrols is the safety of school children, they provide some of the most constructive of police-juvenile contacts.

Departments employing five men or less characterize the police administration of well over one-third of California's cities. Largest cities employ an average of 1.7 full-time persons for each 1,000 population.[11] Cities of 100,000 to 250,000 have the lowest ratio of police to population, 1.2. Cities of less than 5,000 average more than 2 policemen per 1,000 population, as does Los Angeles, the largest city.

The length of a policeman's work week tends to vary inversely with the population of the city employing him. Larger cities most frequently have 40- to 44-hour work weeks; the intermediate cities, 48-hour work weeks; and the smallest also usually 48-hour work weeks, but with many instances of longer weeks totaling as much as 72 hours. Chiefs of police are generally appointed by the manager in council-manager cities, and by the council in most others. In a limited number of cases the chief is appointed by a police commission or elected by the people.

Fire.—The aims of a municipal fire department are to prevent fires from starting and, when they do occur, to extinguish them as promptly as possible. Fire prevention is now recognized as one of the most important functions of a department, particularly as it is becoming evident that such work can reduce fire losses materially. Business and industrial establishments may receive regular inspections, and residences are commonly inspected on request or complaint. Licenses and permits are required for installations which involve fire hazard, and fires are investigated for cause in order that future occurrences may be avoided. Educational campaigns are undertaken to acquaint the public with the necessities of fire prevention.

In its regular fire-fighting capacity a department must maintain the necessary men and equipment in readiness at all times to extinguish fires occurring anywhere within the city limits. In larger cities fire stations must be maintained at convenient locations throughout the area. In practice almost all communities also provide some fire service to areas outside the city limits, either informally or on a contract basis. Mutual aid arrangements are utilized in metropolitan areas, making it possible for neighboring cities to assist each

---

[11] George H. Brereton, "Survey of California Police Departments," *Western City*, Vol. 26 (August, 1950), 31-38.

City Functions and Finance

other in providing fire and police protection when major disasters occur. In addition to the personnel and equipment, a communication or alarm system must be maintained to give immediate warning of the outbreak of fire. Although alarm systems are still necessary, especially in cities depending upon volunteer firemen, in most jurisdictions the telephone has largely replaced other means of reporting fires.

Fire department personnel may be full-time paid, volunteer, or a combination of both. In cities under 10,000 much reliance must be placed on volunteer firemen, and cities under 5,000 depend primarily on such forces. Many larger cities utilize volunteer groups, particularly as reserves to help control major conflagrations. The conditions of employment of regular firemen are different from those of other city employees. Firemen spend more time, usually from 67 to 72 hours per week, at the place of work. A considerable amount of this time is spent waiting in readiness for a call.

Partly because of these peculiarities of fire department employment, interest has been growing in the possibility of combining fire and police activities, and utilizing the same personnel for both functions. Under such a plan all personnel would receive both fire and police training, and would be employed a standard 40-hour week. Certain men would still be assigned primarily to fire service and others to police activity, but all off-duty employees would be available for an emergency requiring either fire or police service. One smaller city estimates that under consolidation a standard 40-hour week can be installed for men performing both police and fire work at a cost 25 per cent less than that of two separate departments both attempting to install such a standard work week.[12]

PUBLIC WORKS

The most common public works functions of a municipality include street improvement and maintenance, provision of sewers and sanitation, and refuse collection and disposal. Other public works activities which may be performed include provision of airport and off-street parking facilities and urban redevelopment. The administration of electrical, plumbing, and building codes is sometimes included in the public works agency. The public works functions may be all in one department or they may be divided up among such units as the street, engineering, inspection, electrical, and parks de-

---

[12] H. K. Hunter, "Sunnyvale Unified Police and Fire Services in One Department," *Western City*, Vol. 26 (July, 1950), 29, 33.

partments. It has been frequently recommended that most or all the public works functions be consolidated into a single agency.

In 1949 municipal public works cost $73,987,000, or 25 per cent of all city expenditures. These funds come from various sources. Allocations may be made from the general fund, and certain special revenues such as state gasoline tax subventions, parking meter receipts, and sewer rentals are earmarked for streets, parking, or sewage facilities respectively. The costs of public improvements may be assessed against property in the vicinity which is considered to have benefited. Funds for the construction of major facilities requiring long-term payment may be obtained from the sale of general obligation bonds which are a charge against the whole municipality. Revenue bonds, which are a charge against the individual facility and its revenues only, may be issued to finance garbage, refuse, sewage disposal, and water supply projects. The Los Angeles Department of Water and Power is pioneering in the use of revenue bond financing. Lease contracts may be utilized under which a private builder constructs the facility and leases it back to the city for a specified period after which it reverts to city ownership.

Streets.—The improvement and maintenance of streets is the most common municipal public works activity, and if public service enterprises are excluded it is the costliest. Municipal street expenditures in 1949 were $48,627,000, 16 per cent of all city outlay, and 66 per cent of the regular public works costs. Funds made available by other governments, primarily the state, provide approximately 50 per cent of the support for the cost of city streets. The gas tax allocation, all of which must be spent on streets, supplies most of this, with a portion coming from motor vehicle license fees and liquor license fees. Traffic fines, which must also be spent on streets, are an important local source of funds. As a corollary to street activities, cities may provide off-street parking facilities financed by revenue bonds, and paid for out of parking receipts. These facilities may be leased to private operators, or, if such a lease is not wanted as a private operation, managed by the city itself.

Sanitation.—Provision of sanitation, one of the basic responsibilities of municipal government, consists primarily of the handling of sewage and refuse. In 1949 this function cost $25,360,000, 8.6 per cent of city expenditures. Adequate sewer service consists of two separate operations which have not been equally developed. First, sewage must be collected from the individual households and industrial locations and transported away, and second, disposal must be made of the sewage. The collection of sewage is governed by well-established principles which are embodied in most municipal systems, although specific difficulties may arise in areas of poor drainage, heavy rainfall, or large population increases.[13]

It is the final disposal of sewage that constitutes the major problem involved in this municipal function. Sewage may be run directly onto the land or into streams, bays, or the sea, either with or without treatment. In some instances sewage is processed by treatment plants which restore the purity of the water sufficiently for it to be used for irrigation. This latter situation is still exceptional, and the widespread existence of water pollution and other nuisances resulting from faulty sewage disposal has recently focused state-wide attention on the problem.

A state program of water pollution control was established in 1949 with passage of the Dickey Pollution Act. Under this law a state pollution board and regional boards have been organized to study the problems, and to persuade, assist, and direct individuals and communities to clean up bad conditions. Also, most of the $45,000,000 appropriated for postwar municipal construction has gone into the building of sewage disposal plants. These two developments should bring about significant improvements.

The collection and disposal of refuse is a municipal function in approximately one-half of the cities.[14] Other methods of handling this need include contract collection, under which a private contractor takes garbage and the city takes rubbish, and private collection, with a private scavenger collecting and disposing of refuse and charging the individual customer directly. Municipal operation is prevalent in the southern part of the state, but in the San Francisco Bay area private scavengers provide most of the service. Although a limited number of cities finance refuse collection and disposal entirely out of taxes, three out of four charge for the service. Interest is growing in the sanitary land fill and high temperature incineration as methods of refuse disposal, because they are clean, convenient, and effective. Although open burning is still the most usual method of disposal, it is rapidly losing favor because of its unsightliness, and because of its contribution to air pollution in metropolitan areas.

Airports.—The provision of airport facilities is an increasingly im-

---

[13] In unincorporated suburban areas the provision of sewage collection systems continues to be a major problem. Contributing factors are rapid population increases outstripping the capacities of existing facilities, and low assessed valuations due to the predominantly residential character of many of these areas.

[14] Winston Updegraff and Richard Bartle, "Refuse Collection and Disposal in 156 California Cities," *Western City*, Vol. 25 (August, 1949), 23–34.

portant public works function of cities in California. There are currently sixty-six municipally owned airports in California, a number exceeded only in Texas. In most cases they are operated directly by the municipality or by a municipal commission, but in some instances they are leased to a private operator.

Financial support for the extensive program of airport construction has come primarily from local and federal sources, with smaller aids being supplied from the state distribution of uncollected refund claims on aviation gasoline.

Urban Redevelopment.—In many cities the redevelopment of slums and blighted areas is gaining recognition as a major municipal responsibility. A community redevelopment agency is activated by council resolution declaring the need for urban redevelopment. A five-man board appointed by the mayor and council governs the agency and proceeds to make redevelopment plans, to acquire, clear, and prepare land for building sites, to provide streets and public utilities, and to lease or sell the property for redevelopment. Persons leasing or buying the land may be obligated to manage it in accord with the aims of the redevelopment program. Under the Housing Act of 1949 the federal government will bear two-thirds of the difference between the cost to buy and clear a site and the price obtainable from an investor. The aim of urban redevelopment is to facilitate the planned reconstruction of slum areas by private financial institutions, chiefly insurance companies. The asssembly and clearance of land and the possible provision of public utilities are the incentives offered investors to get them to direct their funds into areas needing reconstruction.

There is much interest in redevelopment among the largest California cities, and among others that experienced very heavy wartime population influxes. At present, however, the program is only in its preliminary stages and the final outcome cannot be foretold. There are indications that investors may be reluctant to build in the more centrally located slum areas because conditions for monetary return are often better from projects placed on open land near the outskirts or outside the city limits. Possibly the assembly and clearance of land, plus the installation of public utilities, will provide an inducement sufficient to overcome this tendency.

Another important problem faced by the redevelopment program is that of relocating displaced inhabitants, particularly when the redeveloped area will house fewer persons than lived on it previously. This factor emphasizes the need for a close relationship between public housing and the program for redevelopment.

City Functions and Finance 43

MUNICIPALLY OWNED PUBLIC SERVICE ENTERPRISES

A number of additional major services are sometimes, but not regularly, provided by the municipalities for their citizens. These are generally called public service enterprises and include waterworks, electric light plants, wharves, docks and landings, gas plants, and mass transit systems. The operation of municipally owned waterworks is the most important of these services in terms of the number of cities engaging in the activity (181), and in the number of consumers served (substantially more than a million). Approximately 38 per cent of all public service enterprise expenditures go to support waterworks. Although most of these systems were acquired in the early years of the present century, there is current interest in more extensive municipal ownership, as exemplified by the four new acquisitions (all in cities under 2,500 population) occurring during the past four years.

City-owned electric light plants are found in twenty-two municipalities,[15] and serve more than 800,000 consumers. More than one-half of all public service expenditures are taken up by this function, the figure being high largely because of the extensive operations in Los Angeles. None of the systems generates all of its own electricity, and most of them do not generate any, but obtain it by purchase. Municipal acquisition of these plants took place many years ago. Eighteen of them became city owned before 1920, and the most recent in 1932.

Of the other important municipal public service enterprises, wharves, docks, and landings are operated by fourteen cities and absorb 8 per cent of public service expenditures. Five cities own and operate gas plants, the one in Long Beach being by far the largest, and nine cities operate bus systems. These last two services account for the remaining 3 per cent of expenditures on public service enterprises. No information is available as to when the gas plants were built or purchased. Most of the bus systems only recently came into municipal ownership, six of the nine having been acquired since 1939.

A total of one hundred and ninety-six cities report ownership of some type of public service enterprise, and the property involved—valued at $722,015,000—is 62 per cent of the total property owned by all California cities. The expenditures of public service enter-

---

[15] One city, Vernon, leases its plant to the Southern California Edison Company.

prises also bulk large when compared with the regular city functions. These expenditures, in the one hundred and ninety-six cities reporting them, stood at $176,297,000 in fiscal year 1949, and were thus 60 per cent as large as expenditures of all cities on the regular functions.

The enterprises have recorded substantial profits in every year since the end of the depression, except 1948. From 1939 through 1949 the average of their annual profits has been well over one-fourth of their total receipts. In the postwar years this high profit level has somewhat declined, but the utilities' financial condition apparently continues to be sound.

CHARITIES AND CORRECTIONS

Municipal expenditures for charities and corrections, in contrast to those of counties, account for only a small portion of total city outlay. City activity in this field relates primarily to the provision of hospital facilities for emergency cases only. A limited number of cities maintain municipal hospitals, and many of them are run largely on a business basis and pay for most of their services through charges to the patients. In most cities emergency cases are handled through the regular hospitals under contracts or informal arrangements. Only forty-eight cities reported any 1949 expenditures on this function, and the state total amounted to $525,000, or less than 0.2 per cent of all municipal expenditures.

Cities may also provide for low-cost public housing through local authorities appointed by the city council. The authorities sell bonds and receive federal and state aid. The national government underwrites approved housing authority bonds, and makes continuing contributions to maintain the low rent character of the housing provided. The state has also made some contributions, chiefly to assist in providing emergency housing for veterans.

HEALTH

The public health activities carried on by those cities providing their own service are the same as those performed by counties. These are collection of vital statistics, health education, communicable disease control, maternal and child health services, environmental sanitation, and laboratory services. Most cities provide few or none of these services directly, but receive them from the counties. Only thirteen cities maintain their own organized health departments. However, since most of these thirteen are among California's largest, approximately one-half of all city residents are served primarily by municipal departments.

City Functions and Finance

Whenever requested to do so by one of its cities, a county must provide, free of charge, those health services called for by state law and regulations of the State Board of Health. In addition, a city may contract with the county for the latter to enforce the city's health ordinances. The city may repay the county for these services under terms specified in the contract. Municipal expenditures for health services in 1949 were $5,420,000, or 1.8 per cent of the total.[16]

EDUCATION

The educational activities of city governments consist primarily of providing public library service, although a few municipalities make direct contributions to the support of their local school districts. The major aims of local library service are to aid research, to provide information, to serve both formal and popular educational aims, and to provide a source of entertainment. Probably popular education and entertainment are the two purposes receiving most emphasis.

All the larger cities have their own municipal libraries, but many of the smaller cities and towns are served by county library systems through formal or informal arrangements. In other instances residents of unincorporated areas near cities may be served by the city libraries through coöperative arrangements with the county. All these coöperative techniques represent attempts to alleviate the effects of local governmental boundaries upon the provision of library service. They have undoubtedly helped considerably in making some kind of library service available to most of the small towns and incorporated places in the state. There is still dissatisfaction, however, with the adequacy of library facilities and the content of library programs generally serving urban populations. Total city educational costs were $8,310,000 in 1949, or 2.8 per cent of all expenditures.

RECREATION

The recreation function of municipalities includes the provision of playgrounds, swimming pools, recreation centers, and other necessary facilities, and the conduct of a program ranging in content from organized games to community-wide recreation and cultural activities. Children's and young people's games, day camping and longer camping expeditions, folk dancing, social gatherings, hobby clubs, concerts, and art and other exhibits are all rightful parts of a full recreation program. The cities spent $25,378,000 on recreation in 1949, or 8.6 per cent of their total outlay.

---

[16] Significant work of the State Department of Public Health in relation to local health units is discussed in the chapter on county functions and finance.

There is a growing tendency for the city and the local school districts to coöperate in recreation work. The schools' physical plants and facilities are made available after hours and in the summer, and sometimes the schools also contribute to the salary of a recreation director. In many instances the recreation director must thus report to both the city council and the school board. An advisory recreation commission is frequently appointed to assist in formulating policy. Usually this commission is representative of the municipality, but sometimes it also includes representation of the school board. In its area studies, the State Recreation Commission has indicated strong approval of these coöperative recreation programs, and has emphasized the need for further coördination of facilities and activities. It has recommended formal coöperative action under contracts, particularly between cities and school districts, and sometimes also including counties, recreation districts, and other interested units.

FINANCE

Receipts.—Municipal revenues come from a much wider range of sources than those of the counties and special districts. The property tax is the most important single source, and significant amounts of money are also derived from licenses and permits, fines and penalties, privileges, property sale or rental, fees and service charges, sales taxes, parking meter collections, and subventions from other governments. All these sources yielded more than $283 million in 1949. Until a few years ago the property tax provided by far the major part of all city funds—more than 80 per cent in 1932, for example. The difficulty experienced with property tax delinquency and decline of valuations during the depression, the rising expenditures of the war and postwar periods, the increased demands made upon city government, and the relative inflexibility of tax rates combined to require the development of additional revenue sources. Consequently, although the property tax base in terms of assessed valuations grew rapidly after 1939,[17] the tax itself nevertheless continued to decline from its preëminent position in municipal finance until by 1949 it was producing $114,423,000, or only 40 per cent of all city revenues.

Property tax rates in general law cities are limited by state legislation, and those in home-rule cities may be restricted by the local charters. The general state law provides that cities of the sixth class

---

[17] Between 1939 and 1948 the valuations of real estate increased 24 per cent; improvements, 71 per cent; and personal property, 170 per cent. Total valuations increased 60 per cent during this period.

City Functions and Finance 47

may not levy a property tax for general fund purposes to exceed $1.00 per $100 assessed valuation without the concurrence of a majority of the qualified voters. However, a number of special exceptions to this limitation make it possible for a sixth-class city's tax rate to go somewhat over $1.00 without the need of an election. Taxes collected to pay bonded indebtedness are excluded, for example, as are levies to provide an employee pension or retirement plan, to construct flood control works, to pay for sewage facilities, and probably to maintain libraries, museums, hospitals, and veterans' homes, to provide music and advertising, and to supply financial assistance to indigent veterans.[18] By 1950 almost all sixth-class cities had reached the $1.00 per $100 limit on their tax rate for general purposes, and the average total rate for both general and special taxes was $1.32. Most of the $0.32 in special taxes was levied to retire bonded indebtedness. The average for charter cities was $1.62.

Other Locally Collected Receipts.—In addition to the property tax a number of other locally collected funds yielded a total of $107,598,000 in 1949, 38 per cent of city receipts. The various specific sources and their relative importance are indicated in table 4.

Sales taxes, standing at the head of the list, represent the most significant recent development in California municipal finance. Beginning with San Bernardino in 1945, a large number of California cities enacted sales tax ordinances at such a rapid rate that by 1949 the number reporting sales tax collections had reached one hundred and twenty-four, and the total of such revenue provided $25,393,000, almost one-tenth of all municipal receipts. Most cities are levying a rate of ½ per cent, although a few collect 1 per cent.

Fees and charges for services, licenses and permits, fines and penalties, rent and sale of property, and sale of privileges are sources which, although each produces relatively small proportions of city revenues, together provide 24.1 per cent of city income. It is significant that all except one of these sources have grown in relative importance over the past two decades with only the sale of privileges yielding the same percentage of city revenues that it did twenty years ago. Among these sources business licenses probably possess the highest potential for development into a major producer.

Municipal business licensing may be used for regulation and/or the production of revenue. Most charter cities in California and all general law cities are empowered to levy taxes for both purposes, and during the last ten years the trend has been toward licensing for

---
[18] Senate, Interim Committee on State and Local Taxation, *State and Local Government Finance in California* (1947), pp. 318–325.

revenue.[19] The coverage of license ordinances has been extended beyond those businesses and occupations requiring inspection or regulation. In many cases charges of fixed dollar amounts have been replaced by charges measured by gross receipts or by number of employees.

Revenue from special assessments has declined markedly. In 1930 it accounted for more than 16 per cent of all city revenues, but by

TABLE 4

California Cities: Local Non-Property Sources of Revenue

Source	Per cent of total city revenues
Sales taxes	9.0
Fees, charges for services	7.8
Licenses and permits	6.4
Fines and penalties	5.3
Rent and sale of property	2.5
Privileges	2.1
Parking meter collections	1.6
Special assessments	1.6
Other	0.9
Interest	0.8
Total	38.0

1949 it had dropped to 1.6 per cent. This change has been due largely to greater dependence upon fees and charges for specific services, sales taxes, and state assistance for street work. Other minor sources of locally collected receipts include interest payments and parking meter collections, the latter, like the sales tax, being a recent development.

Subventions from Other Governments.—Subventions and aids from other governments, primarily the state, now supply California cities with $61,566,000, 21.7 per cent of their revenues. Twenty years ago this source was practically nonexistent, but the need for additional funds has now raised it to a position of importance second only to the property tax. State aids provide 90 per cent of these funds, federal and county assistance supplying the remainder. The major sources of state aid are motor vehicle license fees, 37 per cent;

---

[19] League of California Cities, *Business License Taxes, A Major Potential Source of Municipal Revenue* (1945) p. 19.

City Functions and Finance

gasoline tax allocations, 31 per cent; local postwar public works funds, 17 per cent; liquor license fee distributions, 11 per cent; and other special aid appropriations, 4 per cent. These funds go largely to support streets (approximately one-third), and the cities' general funds (40 per cent). Assistance is also given health departments, veterans housing, other minor public works, and sewage, the last receiving strong support from the local postwar public works fund.

Expenditures.—City expenditures in 1949 total more than $293 million. One-third of this sum went to provide protection to persons and property, almost 17 per cent for streets, more than 11 per cent into general governmental activities, 10 per cent for interest and debt payments, almost 9 per cent each for sanitation and recreation, and nearly 3 per cent for educational activities. The remaining 8 per cent supported miscellaneous operations, including small payments for charities and corrections. These figures relate to expenditure of all city funds, both those collected directly by the cities, and those provided through various grants and shared taxes. Consequently, a further series of percentages is needed to show functional expenditures of the cities' own locally collected funds. (See table 5.)

It is estimated that almost 12 per cent of the costs of all city functions are financed from subventions and shared taxes. Additional aids to streets, sanitation, and health raise their percentage support by other governments to 51, 37, and 28, respectively, and lower the proportion of locally collected funds that they require. Protection to persons and property, general government, and interest and debt payments, each receiving no important special subventions, are the three functions absorbing the highest percentages of local revenues. Together these three account for almost 60 per cent of all locally collected funds.

During the 1939–1949 decade an impressive increase was registered in city expenditures, a rise of 140 per cent. This figure is approximately equal to the combined factors of population growth and inflation, which account for most of the upward trend in city costs. For example, the per capita costs of government in Berkeley, when expressed in terms of actual purchasing power, showed almost no change during a recent eight-year period. Concurrent gains in departmental efficiency, however, made it possible to give each citizen appreciably more service for the same real expenditure.[20]

Bonded Indebtedness.—The majority of California cities possess a debt limit of 15 per cent of assessed valuation. All of the general

---

[20] John C. Bollens and Stanley Scott, *Effect of Inflation and Growth on City Costs and Services,* University of California, Berkeley, Bureau of Public Administration (1949).

law cities and one-fourth of the charter cities operate under such a restriction. One-half of the charter cities possess no limitation, and the remainder have limits varying from 3 to 25 per cent. In addition to these limitations, a two-thirds favorable vote of the people is required before general obligation bonds may be issued. The existence of overlapping debt created by counties or special assessment districts also frequently operates as a practical restriction on the amount of indebtedness a city may incur.

TABLE 5

California Cities: Expenditure of Revenue Collected Directly[a]

Function	Per cent
Protection to persons and property	35.6
General government	12.7
Interest and debt payments	11.3
Streets	10.1
Recreation	9.6
Miscellaneous	7.3
Sanitation	7.2
Education	3.1
Health	1.7
Special assessment expenditures	1.2
Charities and corrections	0.2
Total	100.0

[a] Subventions going to streets, sanitation, and health were subtracted from the expenditures for each of these functions. Then the other subventions were distributed among the functions on the basis of percentage of total expenditure and subtracted from each respective functional expenditure. Subtraction of these subventions left the approximate actual functional expenditures made from revenues collected directly by the cities.

In most cities the percentage of indebtedness is far below constitutional or charter limits, the state-wide average being 5.8 per cent of assessed valuations. This is one of the lowest levels in twenty years, in spite of a 25 per cent increase in bonded indebtedness between 1948 and 1949. The $423,213,000 in bonded indebtedness outstanding in 1949 consisted of revenue bonds redeemable from the revenues of municipally owned public utilities; bonds issued for harbor, water, light and power facilities; and bonds for sewers, parks, playgrounds, streets, public buildings, and other facilities.

CHAPTER IV

Adjustment of City Areas

Cities occupy a very small part of the total land area of California, but have a large majority of the total population of the state. Incorporated urban places total 1624.2 square miles or about 1 per cent of the area, yet almost 70 per cent of the population lives within their corporate limits. More than 60 per cent of two hundred and forty-seven cities having 1,000 or more inhabitants and for which information is available contain less than three square miles each. There is, however, a tremendous range in territorial size. Several small cities cover only one-fifth to one-half of a square mile while the most populous municipality, Los Angeles, includes 453.2 square miles and is the largest incorporated area in the United States. The relationship between population and size, as illustrated by these extremes, is also apparent in each intermediate population classification. (See table 6.)

FRINGE AREAS

The governmental boundaries of a city and its resulting territorial jurisdiction seldom coincide with the limits of its physical development. This is the fundamental problem of urban area adjustment. As a result, most cities are bordered by unincorporated fringe areas and the larger urban concentrations become parts of complex metropolitan areas. Eight hundred and eighty-five unincorporated areas in California possess place names and constitute almost three times the number of incorporated cities. They range in population from 25 to 42,000. Some are independent rural trading centers, but many are adjacent to incorporated cities of which they are economically and socially a part. Thirty-two of them are more populous than the average general law city and the five largest—East Los Angeles (42,-000), Belvedere Gardens (38,000), Bellflower (34,500), Altadena (32,000), and Bell Gardens (30,000)—are all in Los Angeles County.

Particularly since the 1930's there has been a substantial growth of areas immediately beyond city limits largely at the expense of the cities. During the depression years these fringe areas provided temporary relief from high city rents and from greatly increased city property-tax burdens. Until recent years the availability of mass transportation facilities was significant in determining the direction of residential developments. This importance has been appreciably reduced by the improvement and intensified use of automobiles and roads which have very much enlarged the area in which people can live and still work within the city. Better private transportation means and more and superior paved highways, both more intensively used, have been facilitating the growth of unincorporated areas. Deterioration of certain central business and residential sectors also encourages more people to move outside of the city limits.

Builders are attracted to urban fringes because of the existence of many land tracts often easily acquired at costs lower than those of vacant lands within the city. The high asking price of vacant city property, which frequently constitutes more than two-fifths of the city area, is based upon exaggerated hope of future use and has been a significant cause of fringe development. Other attractions to private builders are elimination of the cost of tearing down old structures, and absence of adequate building and zoning controls. Unhampered by city restraints, large real estate promotions can become highly important stimulants to fringe growth. Industries locating in the fringe can also usually build without conforming to necessary city regulations and their property holdings are not subject to the tax rate of the neighboring city.

The reasons that families settle in outlying areas are numerous. They desire the benefits of more open country and freedom from the noise, dirt, and crowding frequently found in cities. They believe fringe localities are better places to raise children, are less congested, are cleaner and quieter, provide larger lots. Taxes, usually much lower than those of the adjacent city when the unincorporated area is first developed, are accepted without protest, but the new owners may soon discover that lower taxes are directly related to inadequate services.[1]

As an unincorporated area grows in population, its residents find that for their own welfare it is urgent to have police and fire protection, water, sanitation, and other public services. Then, too, the

---

[1] Richard Andrews, "Elements in the Urban Fringe Pattern," *Journal of Land and Public Utility Economics*, Vol. 18 (May, 1942), 169–183; U. S. National Housing Agency, *Land Assembly for Urban Redevelopment* (December, 1945), p. 6; Richard Dewey, "Peripheral Expansion in Milwaukee County," *American Journal of Sociology*, Vol. 54 (September, 1948), 118–125.

TABLE 6
California Cities: Average Areas and Percentage Distributions by Area and Population Class*

Population	Number of cities	Percentage distribution by area class (square miles)										Average area of cities
		Under 1	1-2	2-3	3-4	4-5	5-10	10-15	15-20	20-25	25-30	Over 30	
1,000–2,500	54	50	35	9	4	2	0	0	0	0	0	0	1.19
2,500–5,000	51	25	45	7	4	4	8	0	0	0	0	0	1.86
5,000–10,000	48	12.5	38	17	12.5	10	4	4	2	0	0	0	3.00
10,000–25,000	62	0	19	13	29	8	23	3	5	0	0	0	4.61
25,000–50,000	14	0	0	22	0	0	43	14	14	0	0	7	10.28
50,000–100,000	9	0	0	0	0	0	22	33.5	33.5	11	0	0	13.76
Over 100,000	9	0	0	0	0	0	11	0	22	0	0	67	85.13
Total	247	18.6	29.1	12.6	11.3	5.3	11.7	3.6	4.5	0.4	0.0	2.9	6.58

* Source: Based on U. S. Bureau of the Census, *Areas of the United States: 1940* (1942), pp. 305–306; on annual editions of the *Municipal Year Book*, published by the International City Managers' Association; and on questionnaire information collected by the authors. Several cities are not included in the table because of failure to report to any of the sources or because of recent incorporation.

neighboring city is increasingly annoyed by the effects of insufficient police, fire, and health standards. Urban officials from all parts of California generally agree in their condemnation of neighboring fringe conditions.[2] The city manager of a southern California city characterizes the situation in the adjacent fringe as "inadequate police regulation of gambling and vice, inept fire protection, substandard streets, and loose zoning provisions resulting in too much industrial land." In many parts of the fringe, according to the city engineer of a growing Central Valley urban center, the houses are substandard in construction and placed too close together. Two northern California cities summarize their difficulties with unincorporated sectors in similar terms. "Lack of sanitation in most areas, low subdivision standards on improvements, drainage, trees and lighting, absence of police protection, inferior fire protection, need for recreation facilities, and lack of comprehensive zoning" is the analysis of the city planner of one of these municipalities. The manager of the other city concludes that the non-city territory contains substandard street and building construction, mixed land use, poor or no street lighting, insufficient sanitation, no water distribution system, and poor drainage.

Many times in the early stages of area growth, fringe inhabitants try to get the county to increase certain services, attempt to acquire contracts with the nearby city or private companies, and/or establish single-purpose special districts. Most county money comes from the property tax, a substantial part of which is often collected but not wholly spent within cities. In this way a city may partly support fringe areas through the county fund. San Diego, for example, is contributing 64.8 per cent of the county general fund while benefitting to the extent of only 54.6 per cent.[3] Therefore, serious doubts exist about the equitability of increasing county services to fringes without prior adjustment of the proportionate cost.

A number of California cities have been furnishing water, fire protection, and sewage disposal services to nearby unincorporated urban areas, frequently at contract rates higher than those paid by city residents. However, an increasing number of cities are refusing to furnish any services to outside areas. Agreements between fringes

---

[2] Based on questionnaire information collected by the authors in coöperation with the International City Managers' Association. A detailed investigation of a California city and its fringe may be found in James W. McGrew and Arthur B. Winter, *A Study of the Fringe Areas of Modesto, California,* University of Denver, Department of Government Management (September, 1948).

[3] Public Administration Service, *City-County Fiscal Relationships in San Diego County, California* (1949), table 5.

Adjustment of City Areas

and private companies are generally selective and sporadic. Garbage collection is the service most frequently supplied by private firms.

Single-purpose districts are also frequently tried as an early expedient.[4] Establishment of such districts often results in more municipal services and more local control than are acquired by an unincorporated county area. But obtaining public services in this manner is a piecemeal process since a new special district must usually be organized to perform each additional needed or desired function. Furthermore, local control of district activities is often illusory. Certain state laws permitting creation of specific types of districts require the county board of supervisors to serve as the governing council. Such governmental units offer no more local control than is attained by unincorporated areas. Many kinds of districts, however, elect directors from the area served. Since most of these directors are seldom opposed in an election, local control may be quite remote. If there is election opposition, by the time four to eight sets of candidates are added to an already overcrowded ballot, popular control has become so diffused that it is almost impossible to maintain. Is it surprising then that citizens generally have far less interest in the affairs of a special district than in those of a city?

Several weaknesses inherent in special districts are absent from cities. Services scattered among numerous districts cannot be planned and financed on a coördinated basis. Districts rely much more heavily than cities on a property tax revenue structure. No two cities can occupy any part of the same area whereas districts are frequently pyramided upon the same territory, thus financially overburdening property.

The shortcomings of districts currently require a choice between incorporation and annexation in any attempt to attain satisfactory urban government. However, fragmentary municipal services or unsatisfactory popular control is not the compelling reason why certain unincorporated areas do, and why many others should, turn to incorporation or annexation rather than to the other alternatives. It is the need for regulation and control of land use, subdivision development and design, and building standards. Only a few unincorporated areas are fortunate enough to be located in a California county that has taken action to satisfy this need. Conversely, when an area does incorporate or annex, zoning, building standards, and

---

[4] Special districts of this type should not be confused with multipurpose intercity or intercounty districts or authorities which, if properly constituted, may offer the most feasible approach to solving regional problems in certain metropolitan areas. See John C. Bollens, *The Problem of Government in the San Francisco Bay Region* (1948), pp. 122–125.

equitable subdivision controls are possible as part of the city's ordinance power.

In California, the decision to incorporate, annex, or remain unincorporated is a matter of local initiation and determination subject to standards determined by state law. The choice by a specific fringe area between these alternatives is dependent upon local conditions, and under existing policy the answer must come from the judgment of the people immediately concerned. Residents of an unincorporated area can accurately evaluate their situation if they will take the time to make a careful study based upon complete information. A representative committee charged with determining the facts and reporting its findings to the entire fringe community must be organized. It should be composed of proponents and opponents of the alternatives (when such advocates exist), large and small property owners, representatives of other communities that will be affected by the action taken locally, and business, labor, and farm interests.

A definite plan of action can then be followed. Full information about the unincorporated community should be collected, and a complete description prepared. Tentative or alternate boundaries should be shown, present and future population estimated, social and economic characteristics reviewed, and present and probable future assessed valuation tabulated. It should contain also an analysis of the existing governmental organization, including an account of services performed by the county and special districts, costs, tax levies, and the over-all property tax rates of the county and special districts.

Services that the community wants and those currently provided by the county and special districts, and the quality or service level provided and that desired should then be compared. Functions to be considered should include fire and police protection, schools, sewage and sanitation, streets, sidewalks, and street lighting, public health, library facilities, and planning and zoning services. Those that will not be affected by a shift in status should be noted. The probable effect of any change upon property values and utility and insurance rates should be considered.

Finally, a thorough investigation should be undertaken into the means available for obtaining more or better services. Their relative merits need to be weighed carefully in the specific situation, and the probable costs and revenues must be estimated. The main published source of information about the costs and revenues of city government is *The Annual Report of the Financial Transactions of the Municipalities and Counties of California*, issued by the State Controller. The annual county financial report and budget should show

Adjustment of City Areas

the basic cost information on county services and tax rates and the number, function, tax rates, and costs of special districts in the area. Perhaps the best source of information will be the officials of California cities approximating the area under consideration in size and assessed valuation. In forecasting expenditures and revenues preliminary to incorporation or annexation, the additional costs to be assumed by the community because of withdrawal of some county services must be considered in relation to certain direct payments of state funds allocated to cities. Information about withdrawal of county support can be acquired from the county board of supervisors. The State Board of Equalization in Sacramento can supply facts relating to state grants and subventions.

Two points should be recognized in an expenditure and revenue analysis. The types of governmental services rendered vary considerably between cities, and the level or intensity of the services performed differ even more. In considering incorporation or annexation, it is thus important to remember that a city government need engage in only those activities that its residents desire, and a level of service is based upon those desires adjusted to the community's financial ability.

Incorporation.—The legal process of incorporating requires meticulous adherence to all procedural details. Since in the matter of seeking incorporation the initial responsibility rests with residents of the area, they usually obtain professional legal assistance. The basic requirements are that the unincorporated area must contain at least five hundred inhabitants and must not already be incorporated as a city nor be part of an existing municipality.[5] If an area meets these fundamental conditions, it may petition the county board of supervisors for incorporation as a general law city.

The petition must be signed by a minimum of 25 per cent of the landowners whose holdings represent not less than 25 per cent of the total value of the land in the area and it sets forth the boundaries and number of inhabitants. In incorporating, careful consideration should be given to probable population growth and area needs since annexations to a city may be slow in coming. Thus, the question of territorial size should be viewed from the standpoint of the whole community and should not be resolved merely by including the lands of individuals who favor or do not oppose incorporation.

The county board of supervisors receives the petition and checks its validity and sufficiency. The petition is dismissed if either the number of signatures or the boundary description is inadequate. If

---
[5] *Deering's General Laws,* Act 5233.

it is acceptable, the board sets a date for a hearing after receiving payment for the publication costs and election notice. The board, which may decrease but not increase the proposed size, determines the boundaries and number of inhabitants, and gives notice in the area of the special election.

To be successful the incorporation proposal must receive a majority of the votes cast by the elector residents within the boundaries of the proposed city. The first city officials are chosen at the same time. If the election is favorable, the county board of supervisors declares the territory incorporated. When a copy of such an order is filed with the secretary of state, the incorporation is officially complete.

Incorporation is a device that has been used repeatedly in California for acquiring additional or intensified urban services. The greatest period of growth in number of cities occurred between 1900 and 1920 when one hundred and thirty-seven of them came into legal existence. This was seventeen more than were created in the fifty-year period beginning in 1850. In the thirty years since 1920, fifty-one urban areas organized, or less than half as many as did during the previous twenty years. However, with the recent population growth and anticipated future trends the rate of city incorporation may increase.

In spite of the concentration of 70 per cent of its inhabitants in incorporated places, California has a small number of cities in comparison with other states. It trails North Carolina and North Dakota and ranks twentieth nationally. Although containing about 8 per cent of the national urban population, it has only 2 per cent of the incorporated areas. Furthermore, cities in California are highly concentrated in a few sections. There are no active cities in Alpine, Mariposa, Mono, or Trinity counties. Eleven other counties contain only one municipality each. In contrast, eight urban counties include one hundred and twenty-two cities, or 40 per cent of the total.

California cities have been brought into legal existence for a large number of reasons. An unincorporated area is dependent upon the county board of supervisors rather than on the will of the people of the community itself. Residents of the area may feel that the county board is unresponsive to their needs. By incorporating, they substitute local coördinated control by a city council for control by county and/or special district officers.

There are several specific reasons that may motivate individual incorporations. One is the desire for new services or for higher levels of service than the county or single-purpose special districts are willing or able to give. Also important is the need for regulation to pre-

Adjustment of City Areas

vent nuisances, and to permit the orderly and economical future development of land uses. Demands for adequate planning, zoning, and building regulations have often prompted communities to incorporate. Less frequent, but still significant in certain instances, is the desire for special advantage. A prominent example is the incorporation of a small area with a low level of service at the borders of a metropolitan city in order to limit the central city's growth and thereby escape its taxes.

An incorporated place has several advantages over an unincorporated area. Incorporation permits local affairs to be controlled by the persons most directly interested and affected. A city is a multifunctional unit of government with an ordinance power sufficiently broad to meet most local problems as they arise. Incorporation is a governmental device that permits comprehensive community planning. It can result in governmental simplification if used as a substitute for or as an alternative to the special district method, for a primary task of city government is to integrate activities and services. The two most substantial arguments raised against individual incorporations are: (1) annexation may be more in keeping with the needs of the area of which the unincorporated community is a part, and (2) the taxable resources of the unincorporated place may not be sufficient to finance the cost of desired city government services.

Annexation.—The annexation of inhabited unincorporated territory to an existing city also involves a detailed legal process.[6] The initial step requires a petition favoring annexation, to be signed by not less than one-fourth of the qualified voters residing within the area. After receiving this petition and unless a majority of the owners of separate parcels of property in the area file written protests, the council of the city to which the annexation is proposed must immediately call a special election in the area. The question of annexation is voted upon in the area after a minimum of fifty days' notice. If the special election results in a favorable majority vote of the residents of the territory, the council of the annexing city may approve the annexation by ordinance. Failing to do so, the council must submit the question to the voters of the annexing city.

Upon passage of the ordinance, or following a favorable majority vote, the official documents are filed by the clerk with the secretary of state. The annexation is legally complete on the filing date. When an unincorporated area is considered uninhabited because it has fewer than twelve registered voters, either the city council or the property owners in the unincorporated area may start annexation

---

[6] *Deering's General Laws,* Act 5159.

proceedings, no election being necessary, and the decision of the council determines the outcome of the proceedings.

Annexation is a very active movement in California. Forty-eight cities in the San Francisco Bay area together completed more than three hundred annexations since 1900. This acquisition of 139 square miles doubled their total area. The most prominent example of the growth of a single city through annexation is that of Los Angeles which now encompasses more than 453 square miles. Its areal growth is still continuing. Since 1948 it has absorbed slightly more than one square mile. California's second city in territorial size, San Diego, is also still growing, having made land acquisitions of about three and one-half square miles in the last two years. It now contains almost 100 square miles.

Eight other cities—Compton, Coronado, Fresno, Monterey, Napa, Palo Alto, Sacramento, and San Jose—individually annexed more than one square mile in the two-year period of 1948–1949. In fact, cities of the two largest states, Texas and California, which are experiencing big population gains, especially in urban areas, easily lead all other states in the total number of these substantial annexations completed since 1944. However, most annexations in California and elsewhere are small. For example, forty-one of the forty-nine California cities that made annexations in 1949 absorbed less than one-fourth square mile each. Then, too, all recent California municipal annexations have involved the acquisition of unincorporated land by an incorporated city. It is thus apparent that annexation is continuing to be an important means of confronting the problems of fringe areas.

Various reasons prompt the city and the fringe area to want annexation. For many cities it is the desire to direct the development of adjacent areas through planning controls. It is often felt that annexation is the only immediate way of facilitating the coödination of neighboring areas into a needed community pattern. Some cities advocate absorption so as to compel outlying areas to pay their equitable portion of the cost of benefits they are receiving. Cities seldom want annexation solely to achieve a larger population and greater revenue. The main inducement for most fringe areas to favor annexation is the possibility of obtaining more and better services.

Most opposition to specific annexations emanates from the unincorporated areas, and an anti-annexation campaign is usually built around fear of higher taxes and concern over building restrictions. Occasionally fringe hostility develops because the city has failed to supply adequate information to fringe residents so that a considered judgment could be formed. City annexation resistance is generally

Adjustment of City Areas

derived from either the belief that the area will be an undue tax burden or the desire to have services increased in certain city sections rather than extended to the territory that might be annexed.

Annexation programs and policies, when intelligently formulated and properly used by California cities, have proved notably worth while and effective. An adequate city annexation program must consist of collecting detailed facts about the fringe and its relationships with the city, considering the effect of current and probable future fringe developments in planning the city, making certain that city finances are ample to render services promptly, taking the initiative in presenting accurate data to the outlying area on comparable costs and services, and developing mutual understanding between the city and the fringe.

There is also considerable agreement about the features of a generally applicable annexation policy. Annexations should be general and not selective. The city must accept leadership in working out the problems of the city-fringe community. Annexation should preferably be undertaken when the fringe is becoming urbanized and first needing city services and before it is substantially developed. And finally, municipal expansion must conform to the requirements of sound financing and well-balanced, over-all development.

METROPOLITAN AREAS

A less common, yet more serious area adjustment difficulty than that of fringe areas is found in various sectors of the state where there are densely populated clusters of cities and unincorporated urban areas confronted with major problems requiring intergovernmental solutions. There are six such metropolitan areas in California centering around the core cities of Fresno, Los Angeles, Sacramento, San Francisco–Oakland (including San Jose), Stockton, and San Diego. The Los Angeles metropolitan area is the largest in the state, in both population and area and the third most populous in the United States. The Stockton and Fresno areas are smallest in population and area, respectively. The newer methods of transportation and communication have been particularly important in welding many neighboring communities together into such larger physical units requiring area-wide governmental action.

Metropolitan areas in California are growing rapidly in both population and area. Furthermore, incorporated and unincorporated urban areas surrounding the central cities in each of these metropolitan areas have generally had greater proportional population gains in recent decades than either the metropolitan area as a whole or the central cities. This general metropolitan population growth has increased the number of personal contacts and has aided metropolitan areas to become more closely knit, economically and socially. But at the same time, the regions have expanded in size and the population growth has been distributed among more local governmental units. The end result has been a multiplication and intensification of regional problems.

The quantity and quality of many services provided by an individual city become intercity matters when a number of urban places develop in proximity. Sanitation, water, public health, fire and police protection, and recreation are several matters about which difficulties usually arise in both metropolitan and fringe areas. However, because metropolitan areas are larger in territorial size and contain a more complicated system of governmental units, their functional shortcomings are more acute.

Transportation, which is tremendously important to the well-being of any urban area, is the most aggravated metropolitan shortcoming in California.[7] Mass transit operations are now in a critical period of declining passenger revenues and repeated fare increases. Greater use of private vehicles resulting largely from the growing inadequacy of mass transit brings up in turn a number of problems which are as yet unsolved. Metropolitan transportation is generally characterized by low intercity mass transit speeds, caused by inadequate equipment and surface lines, lack of mass transit in certain parts of the metropolitan area, insufficient freeways and airports, and inefficient terminal facilities, including parking accommodations. The need for day-to-day movement of people has outrun attempts to solve these problems on an individual city basis. It is not the unrealistic city or county boundary so much as the time and cost of travel that limit the extent of metropolitan areas.

Not only are such area-wide problems found in large numbers, but also it is difficult under the existing system for people to plan and effect adequate solutions. On election day voters in a metropolitan area are asked to make intelligent decisions on a bewildering variety of issues and candidates. Even if these voters, who most often are residing simultaneously within the jurisdictions of a city, a county, and numerous special districts, succeed in becoming informed on local governmental issues, they can seldom vote on area-wide problems. Instead they are generally limited to voting on a segment of an important matter which concerns the entire metropolitan area. If the voters of a large city in the metropolitan area feel,

---

[7] For recent evidence, see Assembly, Interim Committee on Public Utilities and Corporations, *Preliminary Report on Rapid Transit for the Los Angeles Area* (April, 1950).

Adjustment of City Areas

for example, that it is urgent to improve the condition of regional transportation, they can make a decision at the polls which will affect only a part of the area that should be concerned with the problem. Furthermore, voters of another part of the area may approve a proposition which runs directly counter to the one passed by residents of the first city. Voters of any one section of a metropolitan area thus have no control over a great many local governmental units dealing with limited phases of comprehensive problems. Having realized the difficulty of working for solutions through local election devices, citizens and officials of California's metropolitan areas are trying other approaches.

Annexation.—There have been a variety of efforts to solve California metropolitan problems. They may be grouped under five large headings: (1) annexation, (2) joint efforts, (3) transfer of functions to other governmental units, (4) the consolidated or federated plan, and (5) regional special districts. Although annexation continues to be the means most often used by California cities to reduce their fringe problems, it is not currently of major consequence in meeting the urgent needs of metropolitan areas. Many cities within the six metropolitan areas are continuing to complete annexations that result in minor simplification of the governmental complexity. However, the central cities that have been most active in recent annexation proceedings—Fresno, Los Angeles, and Sacramento—have each absorbed only about one square mile in the last two years, and San Francisco, which is restricted under existing state constitutional limitations, has completed no annexations since 1856. Furthermore, during the last fifty years almost all annexations in California metropolitan areas have involved the absorption of unincorporated territory by an individual city. Two cities have seldom merged their governmental jurisdictions. Annexations in the six metropolitan areas are thus having little appreciable effect in remedying the present difficulties.[8]

Joint Efforts.—Many joint efforts have been tried or are under way in California metropolitan areas. These may involve joint short- or long-range handling of a problem by two or more local governments, or area-wide concern by individuals working through private or public agencies. They generally relate to activities such as public works, public health, fire protection, law enforcement and planning.

Some are quite short-lived, terminating usually with study or

---

[8] However, annexation is very significant in the Texas metropolitan areas of Fort Worth, Dallas, and Houston. After earlier annexations by Fort Worth and Dallas of 35 and 39 square miles, Houston annexed 79 square miles of unincorporated land in 1949.

solution of the immediate problem at hand. Recent examples of joint efforts of short duration are a low level tunnel survey undertaken by two cities, a subaqueous tunnel commission sponsored by two cities and a county, and a sewage survey financed by six cities. Other combined efforts seem to be more permanent. They include exchange of milk inspection services among cities; sewer contracts between cities or in conjunction with sanitary districts; stand-by fire service among cities, counties, and fire districts; and arrangements among cities for the operation of a police radio station. Other seemingly permanent recent illustrations are a voluntary contract between a city and a county to create a civic center authority; agreement by the state, a county, and a city to restore and protect a seriously eroded shoreline; reciprocity of library services between a county and a city; and aid from three county departments to small cities for a thorough processing of a complete recreation area.

Several joint efforts are of a different nature and are based on area-wide interest and activities by individuals seeking to arrive at solutions through private or public organizations. Only a few of them have had a sustained existence. Strongest among the privately sponsored attempts in the San Francisco Bay area have been the Regional Plan Association which was active from 1924 to 1930 and the San Francisco Bay Area Council which has been functioning since 1945. Like its predecessor, the currently operating organization seeks to increase regional consciousness and understanding through research and through meetings of local citizens and officials.

Permissive legislation authorizing the creation of public regional planning commissions went into effect in 1927. Since 1937 it has been mandatory under state law that such commissions be established in certain areas. With the exception of Los Angeles County where the regional planning commission is synonymous with the county planning commission, no steps toward establishing such agencies have been taken except for a brief endeavor in the San Francisco Bay area in 1941. The Los Angeles Regional Planning Commission advises and makes recommendations to the county board of supervisors concerning the orderly growth of the county. The commission through its studies and services has brought about an important degree of coöperation among the county and various cities in the county. Because the regional planning commission and the county planning commission are the same agency, much of its activity, such as in land-use zoning, is devoted to the unincorporated areas. It has also been recently concerned with master plans for highways, freeways, and airports. The various kinds of joint efforts have helped to lessen public regional obstacles. In the past, however, they have not gener-

Adjustment of City Areas

ally been used regularly and comprehensively enough to lessen or remove many pressing difficulties.

Transfer of Functions.—Transfer of functions to other governmental units is occurring regularly in Los Angeles County, which constitutes the major portion of the Los Angeles metropolitan area, and less frequently in the other five metropolitan areas of California. Currently more than two hundred contracts calling for the performance of a specific function by one unit for another are in operation in the Los Angeles area, which appears to be making greater use of them than any other region in the United States. Every major function of local goverment with the exception of police, purchasing, and public welfare, is involved in at least some of these arrangements.

Although most of the Los Angeles area contracts are between the county and a city, the City of Los Angeles has sewage disposal and water supply agreements with near-by municipalities, and the State Personnel Board provides local units with general technical services and examination work in the field of personnel administration. The county has entered into arrangements concerning tax assessment and collection, health, personnel, libraries, fire protection, planning and inspectional services, streets and highways, and recreation.

The greatest number of county contracts relate to tax collection and assessment, libraries, and public health. Forty of the forty-five cities in Los Angeles County have delegated tax assessment and collection to the county assessor and the county tax collector. The City of Los Angeles did so in 1917. Among the large cities, only Long Beach and Pasadena have not signed agreements. In addition, instead of maintaining separate libraries, twenty cities in Los Angeles County pay a tax rate, designated by state law, to the county in exchange for which the county maintains local library facilities. Any school district may make the school library a branch of the county library and eighty-three school districts have used this option.

Contracts in the field of public health have been facilitated through the adoption of state legislation permitting any city to request that the county perform basic health services. Any city which desires more than fundamental services can contract with the county health officer for the enforcement of designated local ordinances. Forty of the forty-five cities in Los Angeles County have requested the performance of basic health services by the county. Thirty-eight of these forty cities have also signed contracts with the county for the administration of certain ordinances not included within the minimum service.

Transfer of functions to the county or to the central city is largely limited among California metropolitan areas to the experience in

Los Angeles County. Local observers feel that such arrangements are serving a highly useful administrative purpose and may be the forerunners to consolidation or federation of cities. Although there have been occasional lapses of activity in intergovernmental agreements in Los Angeles County, there has never been a period of large withdrawal, and it is likely that there will be considerable expansion of contractual relationships in the immediate future.[9] Additional experimentation with this technique of functional consolidation with a county or a central city might prove fruitful in the other metropolitan areas.

The two most prominent examples of assumption of a function by another governmental unit in the San Francisco Bay area both involve the state. The oldest existing transfer relates to port activities conducted within the jurisdictional limits of the city-county of San Francisco. The port was municipally controlled until 1863. From 1863 to 1874 there was dual state-local control since the state law passed in 1863 provided for a port governing board of three members, one to be elected on a state-wide basis, a second to be chosen by the state legislature, and the third to be determined by the San Francisco voters. The state assumed sole management of the port in 1874 when the state law was amended to stipulate that the three harbor commissioners should be appointed by the governor. They are currently selected by the governor with confirmation by the state senate, and serve indefinite terms.

The more recent example of state activity on a regional problem is the San Francisco–Oakland Bay Bridge. Interest in spanning San Francisco Bay from San Francisco to Oakland was expressed as early as 1848. However, it was not until 1916 that public agitation grew very strong. In the next few years many private individuals attempted to acquire franchises. A state law passed in 1929 created the California Toll Bridge Authority consisting of the governor, lieutenant governor, directors of the state public works and finance departments, and chairman of the state highway commission. This agency was given general authorization to direct the state public works department to construct toll bridges and toll highways and to arrange for financing through revenue bond sales. More specifically, the bridge authority was permitted to construct a highway crossing

---

[9] Frank M. Stewart and Ronald M. Ketcham, "Intergovernmental Contracts in California," *Public Administration Review*, Vol. 1 (Spring 1941), 242–248; Judith N. Jamison, "Neighboring Areas Join Hands," *National Municipal Review*, Vol. 35 (March, 1946), 111–114. The Bureau of Governmental Research, University of California, Los Angeles, has prepared an extensive series of studies on intergovernmental contracts in Los Angeles County.

from San Francisco to Alameda County. Construction of the San Francisco–Oakland Bay Bridge was begun under the auspices of the toll bridge authority in 1933 and completed in 1936 at a cost exceeding $73 million.

The soundness of vesting control of port activities in the state rather than in a local authority, and placing bridge construction in the hands of the state instead of an intercounty district, such as the Golden Gate Bridge and Highway District, is dependent upon the citizen attitude regarding the importance of working out solutions to metropolitan problems at the local level. It is conceivable, however, that unless local governments work out among themselves the acute problems directly affecting them, an increasing number of functions will be assumed by the state government. The realization of this possible result of inactivity may prompt local governmental units to lay aside differences and act together comprehensively.

Consolidation and Federation.—Although intensive study of city-county consolidation and separation was made in the Los Angeles area in the early 1930's, the longest consideration of consolidation has been occurring in the San Francisco–San Mateo sector of the San Francisco Bay area; and another part of the bay area, Alameda County, is the only place in California where the federated proposal has ever been put to a popular vote. As originally constituted by the state legislature in 1850, San Francisco County extended about thirty miles down the peninsula, and provision was made for separate city and county governments. The county retained its original size for only six years. The pressure of a corrupt and inefficient city government brought on legislative action in 1856 when San Francisco city and county governments were merged and the southern part of the original San Francisco County became San Mateo County.

During the latter part of the nineteenth century the City and County of San Francisco began to experience an intensive population growth, and San Mateo County one of more moderate proportions. As a result, many problems arose which required an intercounty solution. By 1923 the first movement for consolidation of the two counties and the establishment of a borough system for the existing cities got under way. A comprehensive report, *The San Francisco–San Mateo Survey*, was prepared by the San Francisco Bureau of Governmental Research under the sponsorship of the San Francisco Chamber of Commerce and released in September 1928. The main elements of the plan were that:[10]

---

[10] San Francisco Bureau of Governmental Research, *The San Francisco–San Mateo Survey* (1928), p. 176.

1. The two counties and the incorporated cities consolidate under a city-county form of government.

2. In the charter to be voted on to effectuate consolidation, the boroughs should be delineated and organized within the city-county for the local control of local legislation, taxation, policies, and administration.

3. Borough representation on the city-county legislative body should be equitably provided.

4. As part of the consolidation question to be voted upon, borough taxation for local borough purposes should be effectively provided, city-county taxation powers for the purposes of the area as a whole should be specifically stated, and both should be properly limited and made subject to popular control of local and area voters, respectively.

5. Any incorporated city or town voting against consolidation (if consolidation is effected by a majority vote of each county separately) should retain its status as an independent municipality, but should become part of the consolidated city-county for the purposes of carrying out county functions for such city.

The bureau report concluded that, if possible, all of San Mateo County should be included in the consolidation, for no natural lines of demarcation had been discovered within San Mateo County beyond which the benefits of consolidation could not be extended. City-county consolidation with a borough plan for control of strictly local policies and functions was felt to be the only workable type of unification for the two counties.

Liberalized state enabling laws relating to consolidation were enacted in 1929. Consolidation provisions were submitted in duplicate as amendments to the old San Francisco charter and as part of the new charter in 1931. Both were approved by the San Francisco voters with the charter amendment passing by almost four to one. With the mechanics of consolidation made an integral part of the San Francisco charter and with essential state enabling legislation passed, successful completion of the consolidation movement seemed finally in sight by mid-1931. But strong opposition in San Mateo County suddenly crystallized and a home-rule charter for San Mateo County was adopted by the voters in the following year. The peak period of interest in consolidation, from 1928 to 1932, elapsed without the San Francisco–San Mateo County consolidation proposal ever being brought to a vote in the two counties. Interest in the consolidation of San Francisco with San Mateo, Alameda, or Marin counties has subsequently developed several times, but has never been sustained for more than a few months.

Adjustment of City Areas

Earlier, in 1921 and 1922, somewhat similar proposals calling for a federated city-county consisting initially of all of Alameda County, and later of only a part of the county, were rejected by voters of the areas concerned. The plan was revived briefly in 1934. The consolidated or federated approach to solving metropolitan problems has been often highly recommended, but because of its political unpalatability it is unlikely to be tried in any California metropolitan area in the foreseeable future.

Regional Special Districts.—Wide use of the special district device in metropolitan areas of California has been facilitated by the large amount of relevant state enabling legislation. Five examples are indicative of the importance of special metropolitan districts. The Metropolitan Water District of Southern California provides water for cities and water districts in a three-county area extending from Los Angeles to San Diego. The East Bay Municipal Utility District supplies water to nine cities and numerous county water districts and unincorporated areas in the East Bay sector of the San Francisco Bay area. The East Bay Regional Park District, formed by the joint action of seven East Bay cities, furnishes a regional network of park areas. The Golden Gate Bridge and Highway District (which encompasses all of five San Francisco Bay area counties, all of Del Norte County which borders the Oregon state line, and part of Mendocino County) constructed and now operates the bridge spanning San Francisco Bay from San Francisco to Marin County. The Sacramento Municipal Utility District, which began operations in 1947, distributes electric power to residents of cities and unincorporated areas in a 653-square-mile region in and about metropolitan Sacramento. There is a mounting interest in more extensive application of the special district device. It has many merits and it is likely that the idea will spread in the immediate years ahead.[11]

Citizens and officials of California's six metropolitan areas have not been hesitant in discussing and trying various approaches designed to eliminate area-wide problems. Their persistence should not be blunted through disappointment at failing to work out a comprehensive solution up to the present time. A complete answer to this perplexing matter of area adjustment has yet to be realized.

---

[11] Enabling legislation authorizing the establishment of a San Francisco Bay area metropolitan rapid transit district was passed by the state legislature in 1949. *Cal. Stats.* 1949, chap. 1239. Detailed discussions by a state legislative interim committee regarding the feasibility of creating a San Francisco Bay port authority were held in 1950. Further consideration of this approach is contained in Edwin A. Cottrell, "Problems of Local Governmental Reorganization," *Western Political Quarterly*, Vol. 2 (December, 1949), 607–609.

CHAPTER V

County Governmental Organization

County government in California currently operates neither exclusively as an instrumentality of the state nor solely as a unit of local government. It is in transition, with its future course somewhat undetermined. As political subdivisions of the state, counties were established and have developed as local agencies to perform basic functions of general state-wide importance. They were molded around property recording, law enforcement, judicial administration, property assessment, tax collection, and road construction and maintenance. More recently other functions of a dual character which combine state and local interests have been added to the established county services. These include public welfare administration, public health protection, water conservation, flood control, and services to agriculture. There are increasing indications that still other functions, such as parks and recreation, sanitation, and services to business and industry, will soon be generally assumed by counties.

Like cities, the fifty-seven counties of California are grouped into the two broad legal classifications of general law and freeholder charter or home-rule governmental organization. During the period from 1849, when the first California state constitution was written, to 1911, when the county home-rule amendment was added to the constitution, all counties were directed wholly through state laws. During this sixty-two-year period, counties were governed by either special or general state statutory acts.

The principal attention paid to counties by the Constitution of 1849 pertained to judicial organization. Under this first constitution general laws relating to the duties of certain county officers were passed, but the number of special county laws enacted was exceedingly large. In addition to many judicial officials, certain county officers—the board of supervisors, clerk, district attorney, sheriff, and coroner—were named and their elections specified in the first

County Governmental Organization

constitution. Thirty years later, a new state constitution authorized the legislature to create a uniform system of county government throughout the state. The legislature was consequently prohibited from passing any local or special law affecting county elections and activities, but it could still place each county in a separate class for salary schedule purposes. Another state constitutional provision significant to county governmental organization, which went into effect in 1879, enabled the merging of cities and counties into a consolidated government.

GENERAL LAW COUNTIES

The general law governmental organization operating in forty-eight California counties is based directly upon the legislatively created uniform system of county government authorized more than seventy years ago. In instituting this system, California followed the plan of older states and provided for the election of each officer performing an important function. As conditions have changed and new functions have been added, certain original offices have been abolished and several of those retained may be consolidated into a single office. The original basic plan, which may be characterized as a loose federation of independent officers, has been only partly altered in general law counties. The various departments are integrated solely through such control as the board of supervisors can bring to bear upon the diffused administrative system.

The mandatory state constitutional and legislative provisions that require the filling of many offices through elections constitute the most prominent feature of the governmental organization of general law counties.[1] Offices that must be elective in non-charter counties are the board of supervisors, assessor, auditor, clerk, coroner, constables, district attorney, justice of the peace, public administrator, public defender, recorder, sheriff, superintendent of schools, surveyor, tax collector and ex officio license collector, and treasurer. A limited number of other mandatory offices and boards must be filled by appointment or by officers acting in ex officio capacity.[2] (See table 7.)

---

[1] *Cal. Stats.* 1883, p. 301; 1893, p. 366; 1937, p. 2728; *Cal. Const.*, Art. IX, sec. 3; Art. VI, sec. 8.

[2] Boards that may be appointed at the discretion of the supervisors are a civil service commission, a board of forestry, a highway commission, a board of public welfare, and a board of trade. Among the officers who may be appointed at the supervisors' discretion are: purchasing agent, recreation director, county service officer, public defender, milk inspector, librarian, fish and game warden, forester, mineralogist, poundkeeper, and persons or firms to advise in financial, economic, accounting, engineering, legal, or administrative matters.

TABLE 7

General Law Counties: Mandatory Appointed Officers and Boards

Title (citation)	Term, appointment, membership, and qualifications		
Officers			
Agricultural commissioner Gov C § 24300 Ag C §§ 50–53, 55–66	(4)	S	Must hold certificate of eligibility issued by State Director of Agriculture
Health officer H & S C §§ 450–456	(−)	S	Must have degree from medical college of good standing and repute
Probation officer W & I C §§ 630–634	(2)	J	Specified law enforcement officers are ineligible—candidates nominated by the probation committee
Road commissioner Sts & H C § 2006	(−)	S	Must be a registered civil engineer, or found by the board of supervisors to be capable of handling county road work
Sealer of weights and measures B & P C §§ 12200–12206	(4)	S	Must hold certificate of eligibility issued by State Director of Agriculture
Boards			
Education Ed C §§ 301–321	Five members total:		
	(2)	S	Four members, of whom a majority must be public school teachers, and one a high school teacher (if there is a high school in the county)
	(−)	ex	The county school superintendent is secretary to the board
Election commissioners Elec C § 44	(−)	ex	Board of supervisors
Equalization Cal Const Art. XIII, § 9	(−)	ex	Board of supervisors
Law library trustees B & P C §§ 6300–6307, 6345–6346	Five members if there is no municipal court in the county, six members otherwise:		
	(−)	ex	All the superior court judges if there are not more than three in the county; if more, the judges select three of their number to serve
	(−)	ex	One municipal court judge (if any in county)
	(−)	ex	Chairman of the board of supervisors, but the board may appoint a member of the bar to serve in the chairman's place

County Governmental Organization

TABLE 7 (continued)

General Law Counties: Mandatory Appointed Officers and Boards

Title (citation)	Term, appointment, membership, and qualifications
Law library trustees (*cont.*)	(—) S A sufficient number of persons, members of the county bar, to make up a total membership of five in counties without a municipal court, or six in counties with such a court
Parole commission DA 5780	Three members total: (—) ex Sheriff (—) ex District attorney (—) ex Chief of police of county seat

Planning commission
DA 5211c
	Five to seven voting members:
	(—) C Must not be county officials
	Other members (ordinarily nonvoting):
	(—) ex District attorney
	               and
	(—) ex Chief engineer
	               or
	(—) ex Surveyor
	               or
	(—) ex Other officials of the county, one of whom may be a supervisor

Probation committee W & I C §§ 597–606	(4) J Seven members, citizens of good moral character

Key

( ) = term of office, years
S = appointed by board of supervisors
C = appointed by chairman of board of supervisors, approved by board
J = appointed by the juvenile court judge
ex = ex officio

Certain developments have been working over the years toward the goal of at least partial administrative reorganization in general law counties. One trend relates to the authority of the board of supervisors in general law counties to pass ordinances consolidating certain offices into one or more of eighteen specified combinations.[3]

---

[3] *Cal. Gov. Code,* sec. 24300–24303. Although it does not mean a formal consolidation of the two offices, the county surveyor may also serve as road commissioner at the discretion of the supervisors. The surveyor has been so designated in numerous counties. *Cal. Stats.* 1947, 1st ex. sess., chap. 11.

Of the positions that may be unified by the supervisors only those of the agricultural commissioner and the sealer of weights and measures are appointive and not elective. Considerable reduction in the number of elected officials and increased concentration of responsibility among fewer persons who then can be more easily held accountable by the voters can therefore result from widespread use of this power. Two of the optional mergers involve the duties of three officers each: (1) auditor, clerk, and recorder, and (2) assessor, tax collector, and treasurer. The other sixteen alternatives integrate two offices each. The dual combinations that are permitted are listed below. The office in the left column may be combined with the office, or any one of the offices, appearing opposite it in the right column.

Agricultural commissioner	Sealer of weights and measures
Assessor	Tax collector or treasurer
Auditor	Clerk or recorder
Clerk	Auditor, public administrator, or recorder
Coroner	District attorney, public administrator, or sheriff
District attorney	Coroner or public administrator
Public administrator	Clerk, coroner, district attorney, sheriff, or treasurer
Recorder	Auditor, clerk, or treasurer
Sealer of weights and measures	Agricultural commissioner
Sheriff	Coroner, public administrator, or tax collector
Tax collector	Assessor, sheriff, or treasurer
Treasurer	Assessor, public administrator, recorder, or tax collector

After being integrated these offices may later be separated, or reconsolidated in any of the other allowable combinations, by supervisorial ordinance. Persons filling combined positions perform the duties and receive the compensation of the offices involved.

Ninety-five combinations of offices are in effect in forty-six of the forty-seven general law counties. This extensive use of dual and triple consolidations has eliminated ninety-three elective officers and eight appointed officials. Modoc County leads with five consolidations, followed by Calaveras, Del Norte, and Plumas, each of which has four. Thirteen counties have completed three integrations, ten have effected two, and nineteen have one consolidation in operation.

County Governmental Organization 75

Sixty-three or almost two-thirds of the ninety-five consolidations have occurred in the twenty-one general law counties possessing less than 30,000 people. All except twelve of the integrations in counties of more than 30,000 population relate to unifying the offices of coroner and public administrator. Of the more populous counties, Imperial leads with three consolidations. Mendocino, San Joaquin, Santa Cruz, Siskiyou, and Stanislaus have two, and nineteen of the remaining twenty counties have one. Contra Costa, most populous of the general law counties, is the only one without any consolidation of offices.

Thirty-four of the general law counties have consolidated the office of coroner and public administrator; eleven, treasurer and tax collector; eight, agricultural commissioner and sealer of weights and measures; eight, sheriff and coroner; six, auditor, clerk, and recorder; five, clerk and auditor; five, district attorney and public administrator; five, sheriff and tax collector; five, auditor and recorder; three, assessor and tax collector; two, treasurer and recorder; one, sheriff and public administrator; one, district attorney and coroner; one, treasurer and public administrator; and one, clerk and recorder. No county has merged the offices of treasurer, assessor, and tax collector or those of treasurer and assessor or the two positions of clerk and public administrator. (See table 8.)

Other developments affecting the governmental structure of general law counties have been at work for a number of years without much public attention. The addition of functions authorized to be performed by counties, particularly since 1930, has stimulated one of these two trends. Some added powers have been vested in existing independent offices and others have been granted to newly established offices or commissions. However, in many instances, the administration of newly established functions has been allotted to employees appointed by the board of county supervisors rather than to separately elected, autonomous county officers. Frequently the supervisorial board determines whether the function shall be assumed by the county. The over-all effect has been that the increase in functions has meant an increase in supervisorial power and consequently a greater degree of administrative integration and coördination in county governmental activities. The other trend has involved the introduction of staff activities, such as centralized budgeting and purchasing. This development has also contributed to concentration of control and responsibility.

Another trend is toward supervisorial control of many county salaries. Although having had power of appropriation from the beginning, boards of supervisors used it sparingly until the installation

TABLE 8
General Law Counties: Consolidation of Offices*

County	1950 Population	Offices consolidated	County	1950 Population	Offices consolidated
Less than 30,000 population			*More than 30,000 population*		
Alpine......	236	a c i	Contra Costa	297,439	......
Amador.....	9,101	a e i	Humboldt...	68,548	i
Calaveras....	9,850	c f i o	Imperial.....	62,580	g m o
Colusa......	11,567	d i	Kern........	227,163	i
Del Norte....	8,027	b f j m	Kings.......	46,265	i
El Dorado...	16,046	e i	Madera.....	36,763	i
Glenn.......	15,341	i o	Marin.......	85,237	i
Inyo........	11,486	g i n	Mendocino..	40,596	h m
Lake........	11,380	i n o	Merced.....	69,396	i
Lassen......	18,430	b f m	Monterey....	129,911	i
Mariposa....	5,083	b i	Napa.......	46,373	i
Modoc......	9,643	b f j m o	Orange......	214,061	i
Mono.......	2,083	c k l	Placer.......	41,324	i
Nevada.....	19,409	e f o	Riverside....	169,392	i
Plumas......	13,398	e g j m	San Joaquin.	200,535	f m
San Benito...	14,330	a c i	San Luis		
Sierra.......	2,363	a c i	Obispo....	51,115	i
Sutter.......	26,135	f i	Santa Barbara	97,741	m
Trinity......	5,045	a c i	Santa Cruz..	65,920	f i
Tuolumne...	12,517	e f j	Shasta......	36,062	i
Yuba.......	24,251	b f j	Siskiyou.....	30,517	i o
			Solano......	102,750	i
			Sonoma.....	102,774	i
			Stanislaus....	126,765	f i
			Tulare......	148,711	i
			Ventura.....	113,415	i
			Yolo........	40,453	o

* Source: Secretary of State, *Roster: State, County, City and Township Officials of the State of California* (1st 1950 revision), pp. 68–112, 219.

Key

a. Sheriff and tax collector
b. Auditor and recorder
c. Auditor, clerk, and recorder
d. Clerk and recorder
e. Clerk and auditor
f. Treasurer and tax collector
g. Assessor and tax collector
h. Treasurer and public administrator
i. Public administrator and coroner
j. District attorney and public administrator
k. District attorney and corner
l. Sheriff and public administrator
m. Sheriff and coroner
n. Treasurer and recorder
o. County agricultural commissioner and sealer of weights and measures

County Governmental Organization

of uniform budgetary procedures was achieved. Even then control over independently elected county officers was usually negligible since the state legislature determined salaries of these officers and their subordinates. It was only with the passage of a constitutional amendment in 1933 that state legislative power over county salaries was restricted. The boards of supervisors were given the authority to fix the compensation of all county officers and employees except their own salaries and those of the auditor, district attorney, and grand and trial jurors.

An additional important administrative development which may eventually become widespread among general law counties is now operating in Stanislaus and Kern counties. It is the establishment of an appointed executive by the board of supervisors. Although some duties of the two positions are similar, the Stanislaus County administrator has broader responsibilities than the Kern County administrative officer. Both of them focus much of their attention on financial matters. They assist the board in preparing the annual budget and can propose changes at the preliminary and final adopted stages. They are also charged with making recommendations designed to improve county administration. In many ways, however, the Stanislaus County administrator currently has a wider range of activities. This is especially true in terms of recommendations on purchases, capital outlays, personnel transfers, job creation and abolition, and expenditure supervision. The Kern County administrative officer has only limited jurisdiction in these matters. In addition, the Stanislaus County administrator serves as the county personnel officer.

In Stanislaus County, the duties of this administrator are specified in a supervisorial ordinance enacted in late 1950. There is no similar formal legal basis for the administrative post in Kern County. Instead, since 1947 it has simply been incorporated in the annual salary ordinance adopted by the board of supervisors. The authority possessed by this administrative officer is founded upon a general understanding between the supervisors and the various county officials, many of which are independently elected.

It is thus evident that counties preferring to function under the general state laws have several significant techniques at their disposal. The possibilities contained in consolidation of numerous elective positions, allotment of new functions to agents of the supervisors, application of staff activities to more affairs, and control by the supervisorial board of most salaries are all effective in achieving greater coördination and integration of county operations. Furthermore, the installation in two counties of an administrative officer to oversee many activities contains broad implications of a movement toward less diffusion in county government and administration.

CHARTER COUNTIES

The major opportunity available to all counties for realizing comprehensive administrative reorganization is contained in Section 7½ of Article XI of the State Constitution. The provisions of this section, which were added to the constitution in 1911, give all counties the right to draft and put into operation, with the approval by majority vote of the people of the county, a home-rule charter outlining structural organization. Such charters are also known as freeholder charters because they are drawn up by elected local citizens known as freeholders. The adoption procedure consists principally of (1) initiation of the election of fifteen freeholders through an ordinance approved by a three-fifths vote of the board of supervisors or by a petition signed by 15 per cent of the qualified voters of the county; (2) preparation of the charter by the board of freeholders; (3) submission of the charter through the board of supervisors to the county voters at a special election; (4) ratification of the proposed charter by a majority of those voting; and (5) approval of the charter without alteration or amendment by the state legislature.

County home rule has been intensively used in California when compared with other states. Its greatest significance is that it offers every county a chance to have considerable latitude in determining its own administrative structure. There are certain matters that home-rule counties must perform under mandatory state constitutional provisions.[4] A county charter must provide for the compensation and the election at large or by districts of not less than three supervisors nominated by districts; the appointment or election and the fixing of the terms of office and compensation by charter provision or by the board of supervisors of the assessor, auditor, clerk, coroner, district attorney, judges of inferior courts, justices of the peace, license collector, public administrator, recorder, sheriff, superintendent of schools, surveyor, tax collector, and treasurer; the powers, duties, and removal of the board of supervisors and other county officers; the consolidation and segregation of offices and the filling of vacancies; assumption through mutual consent by the county of certain municipal functions of the cities within the county when permitted either by general state laws regulating cities or by city charters; and regulation by supervisorial ordinance of appointment, removal, and number of assistants and deputies and other persons employed from time to time in county offices.

---

[4] *Cal. Const.*, Art XI, sec. 7½.

County Governmental Organization

The state constitution enables county charters to contain certain optional provisions such as establishment of additional offices other than those required by the state constitution and laws, determination of the compensation and method of filling these positions, and the organization, taxation, and indebtedness of county road districts. A county charter can be annulled any time after its passage by two-thirds vote of the qualified electors at a special election called through the submission of petitions signed by 15 per cent of the qualified county voters. After this annulling election, the county would again be under the exclusive jurisdiction of the general state laws. No county has rescinded its charter.

Although charter counties may endow themselves with some extension of functions, the scope of their activities is subject to and controlled by general state laws and the state constitution. The charter provisions must not be in conflict with activities performed by the counties as administrative subdivisions of the state. The exact extent of charter county powers has not been judicially determined, but it appears to be much more restricted than that of charter cities in California.[5] As far as administrative organization is concerned, however, it is apparently possible for a county to draw up a charter specifying the appointment of all county officers by the board of supervisors who would be the only elected officials. One appointee of the board could be a full-time professional administrator or executive responsible to the supervisorial board for overseeing and coördinating all county governmental activities. This governmental form, which contrasts sharply with the diffused administrative structure of general law counties, parallels the council-manager system, which is the type most often adopted in recent years by cities in the United States.

Since 1911, when the county home-rule constitutional amendment was passed by the state voters, ten counties, excluding the city-county of San Francisco, have adopted home-rule charters. The ten counties, the effective dates of their latest charters, and their 1950 populations are: Los Angeles (1913; 4,125,164), San Bernardino (1913; 280,252), Butte (1917; 64,374), Tehama (1917; 19,169), Alameda (1927; 733,999), Fresno (1933; 274,225), Sacramento (1933; 275,659), San Diego (1933; 535,967), San Mateo (1933; 234,080), and Santa Clara (presented to legislature, 1951; 288,938). Three of these counties succeeded in adopting charters only after earlier failures. Charters were defeated in San Diego County in 1917 and 1923; in Sacramento County in 1922; and in Santa Clara County in 1934. A 1948 charter adopted by Santa Clara County became involved in

[5] State Commission on County Home Rule, *Final Report* (1930), pp. 71–72.

litigation over faulty advertising, and, although it was ruled valid in 1950, a new charter has been adopted to replace it. Seven other counties have made unsuccessful attempts at charter drafting. These counties are Napa (1917), Santa Barbara (1917), Mendocino (1932), Kern (1935), San Luis Obispo (1935), Siskiyou (1947), and Merced (1950).

Two important changes in administrative organization and procedure have been put into operation in several counties functioning under home-rule charters. The most basic change is the increased integration of administration brought about through strengthening the appointive power of the supervisors or their agents over a number of county officials who in general law counties are independently elected. This places greater responsibility for efficient administration on the supervisors while enhancing their sphere of jurisdictional control. Los Angeles and Santa Clara counties differ most substantially from the general law counties since their charters limit the elective county positions to the board of supervisors, assessor, district attorney, and sheriff in the one case, and the board of supervisors, assessor, district attorney, and the superintendent of schools in the other. Administrative structure is almost equally centralized in Sacramento County which elects the same officials as Los Angeles County, plus the auditor. In San Diego County three officials who are elected in general law counties—the auditor, superintendent of schools, and surveyor—have been converted to appointive status. The other six home-rule counties have generally followed the traditional general law county pattern in their election of officers.[6] Offices, such as coroner and public administrator or assessor and tax collector, have occasionally been consolidated by a home-rule county, but no home-rule consolidation differs from those permitted counties operating under general laws.

The second major distinction from the customary general law system is present in eight home-rule counties.[7] It involves the appointment by the board of supervisors of an administrative officer

---

[6] Among township judicial officers, constables, who are elected in general law counties, are appointed by the sheriff in Alameda, Los Angeles, San Diego, and San Mateo counties and by the county executive in Sacramento County. Justices of the peace are elected in all home-rule and general law counties.

[7] The position of county administrator, which was created by ordinance of the Alameda County board of supervisors in July, 1950, may evolve into a post charged with certain managerial functions. It is in an early stage and is therefore omitted from consideration here. If the position does so develop, only the least populous charter county, Tehama, will not have had an appointed executive officer. The post was abolished in Fresno County late in 1950.

County Governmental Organization

charged with several or many managerial functions. He is called the chief administrative officer in Los Angeles and San Diego counties, where the offices were established in 1938 and 1947, respectively. In Butte County, he is known as the administrative officer (position created in 1947); in Fresno County, administrative assistant to the board of supervisors (1949); and in San Bernardino County, assistant administrative officer (1948). The position is based upon supervisorial ordinance in the first four counties. In the fifth, San Bernardino, it is founded upon a resolution of the supervisors who subsequently made provision for the job in their annual salary ordinance. County executive is his title in Sacramento and Santa Clara counties, and in San Mateo County it is county manager. These latter three positions were incorporated in sections of the original charters of these counties.

Except for San Bernardino County, these administrative officers chosen on the basis of their qualifications are always responsible to the entire board of supervisors which selects a chairman from among its own membership to preside at its meetings. In San Bernardino County, however, the assistant administrative officer is assistant to the chairman of the board of supervisors, although in practice there are many items for which he is responsible to the full board. This deviation has developed because the board of supervisors in choosing its chairman designates him not merely as its presiding officer but also as its executive agent on a full-time basis for a two-year term. By reason of his selection, he is the county purchasing agent. In addition, subject to regulation and control by the supervisorial board, he has general supervision over all county institutions, buildings, and property. In carrying out these stated duties, with which he is frequently aided by the appointed, professionally trained assistant administrative officer, he is sometimes hampered by the continuation of many independently elected county officers.

Just as the administrative-officer systems in effect in the other seven California home-rule counties parallel the council-manager form of city government, so the San Bernardino County administrative structure somewhat resembles the mayor-council organization found in many cities. This general executive-agent proposal was incorporated in the first charter of San Bernardino County, passed by the county voters in 1912 and approved by the state legislature in the following year. Its adoption preceded by twenty years the installation in 1933 of the first non-elected county executives in Sacramento and San Mateo counties.

All eight administrative officers are appointed under civil service for indefinite terms,[8] but greater formal security has been given to persons holding these positions in Sacramento and San Mateo counties. The Sacramento County executive may be removed by four-fifths vote of the supervisors if they pass a resolution stating the reasons or by unanimous vote without a resolution. The San Mateo County manager can be ousted only by four-fifths vote of the board of supervisors. In Butte, Fresno, Los Angeles, and San Diego counties the position itself could be abolished at any time through a three-fifths vote of the board of supervisors. This is the same vote required for passage or repeal of any supervisorial ordinance. The office could be eliminated in San Bernardino County by not being included in the annual salary ordinance. In the final analysis, however, wide citizen support probably offers the greatest security to the administrator and to the job he fills.

Responsibilities of the County Executive.—This administrative officer has certain important personal appointive and removal powers in three of the eight counties. With the approval of the supervisors, the Sacramento County executive appoints the clerk, coroner (who is ex officio public administrator), engineer (ex officio surveyor), recorder, tax collector (license collector), superintendent of schools, and treasurer. Any officer appointed by the board of supervisors or by the county executive may be removed by a four-fifths vote of the board of supervisors upon recommendation of the county executive. The Santa Clara charter specifically provides that the county executive can appoint and remove a large number of officials, including the building inspector, coroner, clerk, engineer, librarian, recorder, tax collector, treasurer, and purchasing agent, and the directors of medical institutions, personnel, planning, public health, and welfare. The San Mateo County manager chooses, subject to supervisorial approval, a more limited number of officers and boards. They are the board of public health and welfare, building inspector, director of health and welfare, purchasing agent, and recreation commission. He may remove his own appointees upon supervisorial confirmation. No direct major appointment or removal

---

[8] The San Mateo County manager (who became an elective officer under a 1938 charter amendment that changed his appointive status as outlined in the original charter of 1933) was made appointive again in 1949 when the state legislature approved a charter amendment that had been passed in 1948 by about a three to two vote of the county electorate. Since the tenure of the incumbent was not affected by this latest charter change, the county manager did not take office until January, 1951. The county manager, who is the first county administrator to possess this official title, was called county executive until the charter was altered in 1949.

County Governmental Organization

authority has been vested in any of the other five administrative officers.

All eight county executive officers are charged with supervising and coördinating all or some county activities. In Los Angeles County, the chief administrative officer has administrative responsibility for all county affairs.[9] The appointed administrative officers in Butte, Fresno, Sacramento, San Bernardino, and San Mateo counties are responsible for properly and efficiently administering county affairs placed in their charge. In addition, the Sacramento and San Mateo administrators advise their boards of supervisors regarding necessary and proper coördination of functions performed by officials and boards not under the jurisdiction of the administrators. The San Diego chief administrative officer supervises and coördinates county affairs placed in his charge by the board of supervisors, and the activities of other county departments, offices, and boards with the exception of certain elective officials and the civil service and personnel officer. The Santa Clara County charter provides for coördination, by the executive, of the work of all appointive and elective offices.

The use of fiscal controls by these chief administrators is a major method of bringing about coördination of county services. In Los Angeles County the chief administrative officer, who formerly served also as the purchasing agent, acts as the chief budget officer.[10] All departments can be required to submit itemized expenditure estimates to the chief administrator who can propose changes in any part of the preliminary budget. He can also recommend transfer or cancellation of any item in the final adopted budget. The expenditures of all county agencies are supervised by him, and departmental requests for any variation from the adopted budget are subject to his review.

The San Diego County chief administrative officer also has certain budgetary and expenditure controls. He can recommend cancellation or transfer of items in the final adopted budget, and he supervises many expenditures. Furthermore, he transmits to the supervisors approval or disapproval of proposed capital outlay or replacement purchases requested by agencies under his supervision.

---

[9] A comprehensive analysis of the role of this important officer is in Abraham Holtzman's *Los Angeles County Chief Administrative Officer: Ten Years' Experience* (University of California, Los Angeles, Bureau of Governmental Research, 1948).

[10] The chief administrative officer requested in 1950 that he be relieved of his duties as purchasing agent so that he could give his entire time to his managerial functions. This request was granted.

The positions of chief administrative officer and purchasing agent have not been combined in San Diego County, but are held by two separate officers appointed by the board of supervisors.

Important fiscal controls have also been given to the Sacramento County executive. He is charged with establishing a modern uniform accounting and reporting system that requires all county officers and agencies to report to him, when and how he directs, information about their activities, personnel, and finances. This enables the county executive to maintain a continuous audit, and adjust existing and contemplated appropriations to the current actual needs of every county agency. Then, too, the board of supervisors may direct each county officer who is required to file annual budget estimates with the auditor to submit such estimates to the county executive on forms prescribed by him. It is then the duty of the county executive to consult with these officers submitting estimates, so that he may make recommendations to the board. When the board of supervisors receives the tabulation of budget estimates from the auditor, it transmits a copy to the county executive, who makes such written recommendations about revisions as he feels are "in the best interests of efficiency, economy, and service." [11]

Under the Sacramento County charter the board of supervisors may authorize the county executive (1) to provide for each organizational unit in the administrative service a more detailed budget subclassification by functions and activities, and within each object of expenditure a more detailed segregation than that provided by general law; and (2) to allocate proposed expenditures by time periods. With board approval, such subclassifications, segregations, and time periods go into effect. Any proposed transfers of budget items must be authorized by the county executive.

Another duty of the Sacramento County executive is to recommend in writing to the board of supervisors the cancellation of part or all of any appropriations whenever he feels the expenditure is unnecessary or not in the best interests of sound administration. Monthly reports of all fiscal transactions of each officer are sent to the county executive, who may at any time have an audit made of any account. All claims against the county must be sent to the county executive for approval or rejection. He acts as purchasing agent of the county and, at the discretion of the county public schools, he may also serve as their purchasing agent.

The Santa Clara County executive is charged with supervision of budget preparation and is responsible for its administration after

---

[11] Sacramento County, *Charter,* Art. X, sec. 46(c).

adoption. He also advises the supervisors on needs for future expansion of public works and services. The appointed administrative officer prepares a budget summary and recommendations in San Bernardino County. Furthermore, he may propose changes in the preliminary budget, recommend cancellation or transfer of items in the final adopted budget, supervise the expenditures of county agencies, and review proposed capital outlays or replacement purchases. In Butte County, he is the budget director and makes financial recommendations regarding county agencies and services designated by the supervisors. He has no further stated budget or expenditure controls. In Fresno County, he works closely with the county expert who prepares the budget. He may recommend item cancellations or transfers in the final adopted budget and supervise the expenditures of certain county agencies.

The San Mateo County manager has only limited participation in financial matters. He is restricted to examining the budget and reviewing claims against the county. All county agencies required by general law to submit budget estimates to the auditor, who is called the controller in San Mateo County, must also submit their estimates to the county manager for advice and suggestions. The budget, when transmitted by the controller to the board of supervisors, is then referred to the county manager for his recommendations. Claims are presented to the county manager for his approval or rejection. The controller, an independently elected officer in San Mateo County, rather than the county manager as in Sacramento County, prescribes the account forms, requires monthly reports of financial transactions of each officer, and may make or have made a departmental audit. Furthermore, unlike Butte, Los Angeles, and Sacramento counties, where the executive officer is also the purchasing agent, San Mateo County has the two positions separated, although there is close coördination since the purchasing agent is appointed by the county manager.

The other major method of coördinating county activities through a chief administrative officer involves the transferring of personnel and the creation or abolition of positions. The Los Angeles County chief administrative officer may recommend to the board of supervisors and the civil service commission temporary transfers of personnel that he feels are necessary. In San Diego County the comparable officer coördinates the administration of departments placed under his supervision by recommending to the board of supervisors and the civil service commission temporary personnel transfers. During periods involving an excess of work, the Sacramento County executive may temporarily transfer deputies, clerks, or employees from one department to another. The transfer authority of the San Mateo County manager and the Santa Clara County executive is similar to that of the Sacramento County executive. The administrative officers of Fresno and San Bernardino counties may also recommend transfer of personnel. In Butte County, this official is specifically authorized to investigate the qualifications of any person in the county administrative service.

The chief administrative officers, with the exception of the San Mateo manager and the Santa Clara executive, also have specific advisory power relating to increasing or decreasing the number of employees. The Sacramento County executive suggests to the supervisorial board improvements in the administration of elective and appointive offices, including increasing or decreasing the number of employees. The chief administrative officer of Los Angeles County is empowered to make recommendations to the board regarding the creation or abolition of positions. In San Diego County, the chief administrative officer may recommend the establishment of new positions or the elimination of old posts under his supervision. In Fresno and San Bernardino counties he may recommend the creation or abolition of county positions. The administrative officer indirectly possesses this responsibility in Butte County where he may prepare reports on any elective or appointive county agencies. The Santa Clara executive is given general powers to recommend changes for the betterment of the public services.

The two positions created through charter provisions in Sacramento and San Mateo counties are subject to express limitations on their powers. There are seven such restrictions on the San Mateo County manager, five of which are identical with those imposed on the Sacramento County executive. The five are prohibitions against (1) exercising any legislative function; (2) expending money except in pursuance of supervisorial appropriations or authorizations; (3) disposing of any real or personal county property; (4) granting or revoking any franchise; and (5) exercising any power or control over any officer not appointed by him. However, this last curtailment does not prohibit these two officers from making recommendations to the board of supervisors or to any elected or appointed county officer or board regarding more efficient or economical administration. The two additional restraints specifically placed upon the San Mateo County manager relate to creating or abolishing any office or place of employment in the county service and increasing or decreasing the salary of any officer or employee.

A number of other California counties have shown considerable interest in various types of administrative integration centering in

County Governmental Organization

an executive officer who would be responsible to the appointing board of supervisors. This has been particularly apparent since the termination of World War II, and recently there have been detailed discussions of the subject in Contra Costa, Monterey, Riverside, Santa Cruz, Siskiyou, Tulare, and Ventura counties, which range in population from Siskiyou's 30,517 to Contra Costa's 297,439.

There are significant differences between general law and charter counties in California. Partial administrative reorganization can result in general law counties, through supervisorial action consolidating certain offices, through supervisorial control of many county salaries, through assignment of some new functions to the supervisors or their appointees, and through provision of staff services, such as coördinated budgeting, personnel, and purchasing, to county agencies under the supervisors. The supervisors may also create a position for an administrative officer. Comprehensive change under general state laws is impossible, however, because of mandatory legal requirements that many officers be independently elected. This can be surmounted if any county decides to draft its own charter. If the charter so provides, it is then necessary to elect only the supervisors, who can appoint all other county officials. Three of the ten charter counties, Los Angeles, Santa Clara, and Sacramento have drastically reduced their elective officers through adoption of home-rule charters. Excluding the supervisors, only three officials are elected in the first two counties, and four in the last. In either a general law or a charter county, supervisors may appoint an administrative officer to coördinate and manage county affairs that are under the jurisdiction of the supervisors, but such appointments can be completely meaningful only when supervisorial control is not restricted by the independent spheres of action of a large number of autonomous elected officials.

CITY AND COUNTY OF SAN FRANCISCO

San Francisco is a unique local governmental unit in California since it is the only city-county in the state, as well as one of the few in the United States. By special legislative act in 1856 the San Francisco city limits were enlarged and the new city area was separated from the remainder of the county, which became San Mateo County. A consolidated city-county area, the second to be so designated in the United States, thus came into existence. The special state legislation provided that in line with the desire of San Francisco residents to rid themselves of corrupt city officials, numerous officers of the old county should become the key personnel of the new city-county. State constitutional notice was given to the city-county government with the passage of the second California constitution in 1879. In the original provisions of this new constitution it was stated that "city and county governments may be merged into one municipal government, with one set of officers," and that "the provisions of this Constitution applicable to cities, and also those applicable to counties, so far as not inconsistent or prohibited to cities, shall be applicable to such consolidated government." [12]

Another section incorporated in the new constitution of 1879 permitted any city or city and county possessing more than 3,500 people to frame its own charter. San Francisco did not make use of this option until 1898 when its voters approved its first charter. Ratified by the state legislature in 1899, the charter was repeatedly amended during the period of its existence from 1900 through 1931.

The current charter, adopted locally in 1931 and effective since 1932, represents a blending of the terminology of city and county governments. The governing board of San Francisco is known as the board of supervisors. It consists of eleven members, six more than serve on the supervisorial board of any California county and more nearly approximating the size of some city councils. Every two years five or six supervisors are elected at large for four-year terms. The board president is selected from among the members for a two-year period. The mayor, possessing a title common to the chief officials of most cities in the United States, is elected for four years. He has important appointive powers including the selection of a chief administrative officer, a designation used in two counties and several cities of California.

Numerous important administrative changes are contained in this charter which substantially contrasts with the previous basic legal document of San Francisco. Exclusive of the superior and municipal court judges, the number of elective officers is limited to the mayor, supervisors, and heads of six executive departments—assessor, city attorney, district attorney, public defender, sheriff, and treasurer. The various officers are elected for terms of four years at three successive annual elections. The assessor and public defender are chosen the first year. In the following year the voters select six members of the board of supervisors, the mayor, the district attorney, and the sheriff. The election of the five other members of the board of supervisors, the city attorney, and the treasurer occurs in the third year. After a lapse of one year, the sequence begins again. The board of supervisors is restricted to legislative functions and is divested of its administrative duties, which have been transferred to the mayor

---

[12] *Cal. Const.*, Art. XI, sec. 7.

County Governmental Organization

and his appointees, particularly the chief administrative officer and the controller, and to elected department heads.

The administrative structure of city-county government in San Francisco thus includes the mayor, the chief administrative officer, and elective officers heading specific departments. Officials and agencies operating under the jurisdiction of the mayor and the chief administrative officer, and those organized under a variety of specifications are delineated in tables 9, 10, and 11.

The chief administrative officer is the coördinator of ten departments, and may pass upon their budget estimates, which are checked by the controller and may be decreased by the mayor and the board of supervisors, acting independently.[18] He is appointed by the mayor and must have executive ability and experience consistent with such an administrative position. His responsibility for the duties assigned him is to the mayor and the board of supervisors, and his removal may be effected through a two-thirds vote of the board of supervisors or through recall by the voters after he has held office six months. Only two men have held the position since it was created in 1932.

---

[18] Additional details concerning this position are in John M. Selig, "The Chief Administrative Officer in San Francisco," unpublished M.A. thesis, University of California, Berkeley, 1939.

TABLE 9

San Francisco Officials and Agencies Appointed by and Operating under the Mayor

Official or agency	Membership, qualifications, and duties	Term
Art commission	10 members, plus mayor and chairmen of library, park, city planning, de Young Museum, and California Palace of the Legion of Honor commissions ex officio. Of 10 appointed members, serving staggered terms, 7 must be from art professions, nominated by professional organizations, including artist-painter, artist-sculptor, musician, litterateur, 2 architects, and landscape architect. Approves art purchases and building designs on city property.	5 years
Civil service commission	3 members, staggered terms. Appoints secretary who serves at its pleasure. Serves as city employment and personnel department, classifies positions.	6 years
Controller	Confirmed by board of supervisors. Removable by two-thirds vote of supervisors, or by recall. Serves as auditor and chief accounting officer.	—
Fire commission	3 members, staggered terms. Appoints chief engineer, secretary, and physician.	4 years
Harbor commission	5 members, staggered terms. One must be agricultural representative, need not be resident. Controls and manages all city and county properties along harbor. Regulates anchoring and mooring of all vessels. Responsible for wharves. Appoints harbor master as chief executive. (Effective only if state transfers port facilities to city ownership.)	5 years
Housing authority	5 members, staggered terms. Constructs and administers public housing projects.	4 years
Library commission	11 members, staggered terms; 3 appointed each year except fourth year, when 2 are appointed. Appoints secretary and librarian.	4 years
Board of trustees of San Francisco War Memorial	11 members, staggered terms; must be approved by board of supervisors. Appoints managing director and secretary who serve at its pleasure.	6 years
Board of permit appeals	5 members, staggered terms; one appointed each year except fourth year, when two are appointed. Approves permits for businesses. Hears appeals where license or permit is denied by issuing agency, or where a permit granted is opposed by an interested party.	4 years

TABLE 9 (continued)
San Francisco Officials and Agencies Appointed by and Operating under the Mayor

Official or agency	Membership, qualifications, and duties	Term
Planning commission	7 members, 5 serving staggered terms, one appointed each year except fourth year when two are appointed; chief administrative officer and manager of utilities serve ex officio. Appoints city planning director, who has adequate administrative experience and technical training; appoints secretary to serve at its pleasure, and may contract for other specialists; adopts and maintains a master plan.	4 years
Police commission	3 members, staggered terms. Appoints chief of police and police surgeon, who serve at commission's pleasure. Certain major police officials are assigned by commission at suggestion of police chief but all are civil service personnel from within the police department.	4 years
Public utilities commission	5 members, staggered terms. Appoints manager and secretary; supervises activities of municipal railway, San Francisco water department, Hetch Hetchy project, and Mills Field (municipal airport). Power to control and supervise all public utilities of city and county. Commissioners are subject to recall.	4 years
Public welfare commission	5 members, staggered terms; policy-determining and supervisory body over welfare department. Appoints director and secretary.	4 years
Recreation and park commission	7 members, staggered terms, not less than 2 women. Appoints and removes a general manager who appoints and removes with commission approval superintendent of parks, superintendent of recreation, zoo director, and executive secretary to general manager.	4 years
Redevelopment agency	5 resident electors who are not elected officers or employees, staggered terms. Acquires property, develops building sites, and controls land re-use.	4 years

TABLE 10

San Francisco Officials and Agencies Operating under the Chief Administrative Officer

Official or agency	Membership, qualifications, and duties	Term of director
Agricultural department: agricultural commissioner		Civil service
Coroner	Appointed by chief administrative officer but under civil service.	Civil service
Department of electricity: electricity superintendent	Administers electrical system of such city governmental agencies as police, fire, and telephone.	Civil service
Department of finance and records: director	Includes functions and personnel of offices of tax collector, registrar of voters, recorder, county clerk, and public administrator, all of whom are under civil service.	Pleasure of chief administrative officer
Health advisory board	7 members, staggered terms; must include 3 physicians and 1 dentist.	4 years
Department of public health: public health director	Director must be licensed physician with ten years' practice immediately preceding his appointment.	Pleasure of chief administrative officer
Department of public works: director of public works	Includes public works not assigned to public utilities commission, and telephone exchange.	Pleasure of chief administrative officer
Purchasing department: purchaser of supplies	Includes bureau of supplies, central stores and warehouses, and central garages and shops.	Pleasure of chief administrative officer
Real estate department: director of properties	Includes rights-of-way agent, bureau of engineering, and management of exposition auditorium.	Civil service
Department of weights and measures: sealer of weights and measures		Civil service

TABLE 11

Miscellaneous San Francisco Officials and Agencies

Official or agency	Membership, qualifications, and duties	Term
Adult probation committee	7 members; appointed by criminal division of the superior court.	4 years
California Palace of the Legion of Honor	11 trustees, mayor and president of park commission ex officio; vacancies filled through appointment by other trustees. Members need not be residents of San Francisco. Director, secretary, and curators appointed by and serve at pleasure of board of trustees.	
Board of education	7 members, staggered terms; nominated by mayor, confirmed by vote of people at next election. Commissioners subject to recall, or to removal in the manner prescribed for other elective officials. Appoints superintendent of schools for a four-year term and a secretary (offices currently combined). Superintendent appoints all certificated employees with approval of the board.	5 years
Board of examiners	Superintendent of schools and deputies. Recommends to board of education issuance and withdrawal of teachers' certificates.	
Health service board	9 members, staggered terms, elected by members of retirement system. President acts as appointing officer under civil service. Board appoints a medical director to serve at its pleasure. Adopts plan to render medical care to members of retirement system.	3 years
Juvenile probation committee	7 members; appointed by juvenile court judges. Nominates probation officer for approval by juvenile court judges.	4 years
Law library	7 members of bar; mayor, presiding judge, 3 judges of appellate department of superior court ex officio; board fills any vacancies and appoints law librarian and other employees.	
M. H. de Young Memorial Museum	Not less than 11 nor more than 17 appointive trustees, mayor and president of park commission ex officio; vacancies filled by appointment by other trustees. Director, secretary, and curators appointed by and serve at pleasure of board of trustees.	
Retirement board	President of board of supervisors, city attorney, resident official of life insurance company, and officer of bank appointed by mayor; 3 members elected from active members of retirement system. Board may appoint actuary and secretary.	5 years
Steinhart Aquarium	Under supervision of California Academy of Sciences of San Francisco. Government must grant necessary funds for maintenance and operation.	

CHAPTER VI

County Functions and Finance

The validity of any generalizations about county governmental functions in California is limited by the wide variations found in individual counties. The activities of a predominantly urban county differ from those of a county in a sparsely populated mountain region, and both differ from those of an agricultural valley county. However, the dissimilarities existing between the counties of Los Angeles, Alpine, and San Joaquin, for example, relate mainly to emphasis and degree of development of specific functions and to the complexity of the administrative organization required to carry them out.[1] The fundamental array of county functions is practically the same in all parts of the state, although in certain areas some are present only in rudimentary form.

The classification of functions is based on that appearing in the county budgets, and includes general government, protection to persons and property, charities and corrections, highways, health and sanitation, education, and recreation.[2] This classification is generally satisfactory, and possesses the advantage of being identical with that of the state controller's local government finance reports.

GENERAL GOVERNMENT

General government includes most activities and offices that are traditionally associated with the work of the county. The major activities of general government are legislative and executive (county

---

[1] Statements in this chapter relating to county organization for handling the various functions apply fully to the general law counties, and to the charter counties with only a few exceptions.

[2] These functions do not include the work done by special districts, although in some instances such districts are very closely related to the regular county government. Important types of districts are lighting, sanitary and sanitation, fire protection, mosquito abatement, flood control, water, and public utility. These units, along with other similar local governments, are considered in the final chapter.

board of supervisors); judicial and legal (justice, municipal, and superior courts, district attorney, and law library); fiscal (auditor, assessor, tax collector, treasurer); electoral; the handling of special matters affected with the public interest (coroner, public administrator, public defender, surveyor); recording (county clerk); "housekeeping" and custodial functions of administration serving the county offices (purchasing, personnel, and maintenance of buildings and grounds); and planning (planning commission). In 1949 the functions of general government necessitated expenditure of $26 million, 12.5 per cent of all county disbursements.[3]

Legislative and Executive.—The central legislative and executive authority of the county rests in the county board of supervisors, the five members of which are elected from supervisorial districts. This body exercises fiscal control over the county through its power to revise and approve the budget. All county officers and departments, and a large number of special districts must present annual budget estimates to the board of supervisors for review and approval. The board supervises county, township, and district officials with a degree of supervision depending upon whether the officers are appointive or elective. Administrative control over elective officers is largely limited to auditing their accounts, accepting their reports, and directing prosecutions against them for delinquencies. Greater power of control is exercised over officers who are appointed and removed by the board of supervisors.

The board of supervisors may levy general taxes on real and personal property in the county; and special taxes for the redemption of bonds, assistance to fairs and exhibitions, and for promotion and advertising of county resources. In connection with the taxation function, the board performs ex officio as the county board of equalization to adjust inequitable assessments.

The range of nonfiscal legislative powers of the supervisors is large. It includes regulation of the number, method of appointment, and term of employment of county personnel; performance of services for and sale of property to special districts in the county; flood control activities; acquisition of water and its distribution; provision of sewage, garbage, and rubbish disposal facilities; provision of public airports; enactment of health or livestock ordinances not in conflict with state or federal laws; granting of licenses for construction of wharves and piers; operation of county free libraries; agricultural

---

[3] State Controller, *Annual Report of Financial Transactions, 1949* (1950), pp. 230–231. With a few exceptions this volume is the source of all financial data in the present chapter.

experimentation; local census-taking; provision of public beaches and small-boat harbors; operation of public incinerators; and activities to attract residents and increase commerce. These powers are in addition to those pertaining to charities and corrections, highways and bridges, protection to persons and property, health and sanitation, education, and recreation, which are discussed later.

As the executive agency the board of supervisors is expected to supervise and administer all county activities. In practice, however, there are serious limitations on the executive and supervisory powers of the board. In the first place, a large number of county officials are directly elected and are able to operate with little supervision. Under such circumstances the board's authority consists largely of its control of finances.

In the second place, most boards of supervisors lack a central administrative office through which their executive authority can be directed and expedited. The absence of such an office compels the supervisors to concern themselves with many routine details of administration. In several counties some type of executive officer has been provided, and in some other instances the secretary to the board has been given a few of the functions which would be assigned to a general manager. Most counties are not, however, characterized by any marked degree of centralized administration.

Administration of Justice.—The California court system below the district courts of appeal consists of the two levels of superior and inferior courts. Although they are identified with county government, both levels of courts may be considered state agencies for which the county provides services and officers. The superior courts, each of which is county-wide in its operations, are the chief trial courts in the state. They have extensive original jurisdiction as well as appellate jurisdiction over cases brought up from inferior courts. Their judges are elected for six-year terms in numbers depending upon the amount of court business. The inferior courts, before passage and implementation of a 1950 reorganization amendment, included township justice courts, city justice courts, inferior municipal courts, police courts, and city courts. They generally handled small lawsuits and minor criminal cases, and enforced the traffic laws. Their jurisdictions varied somewhat, however, those of the municipal courts being widest. There was also much overlapping and duplication in jurisdiction. The township justice courts were the most closely related to county government, and were manned by judges elected for four-year terms.

The 1950 constitutional amendment simplified the complicated and overlapping structure of inferior courts. It provided for two

County Functions and Finance

types of such courts, municipal and justice, the former to be established in districts containing more than 40,000 population, the latter in districts containing 40,000 or less. The division into districts is effected by action of the county boards of supervisors, with the limitation that no city may be divided by a district boundary, and no two or more cities of more than 40,000 population each may be placed in one district. Each district may have only one court. If these new courts follow the pattern of the previously existing municipal and justice courts, the former will have a wider jurisdiction than the latter, and will be expected to relieve the superior courts of an over-crowded docket.

One district attorney is elected in each county and given the duties of conducting prosecutions for public offenses, serving as the legal representative of the county and the state in civil actions, and giving legal opinions to county and district officers. In addition, the district attorney's powers of investigation have enabled him to operate as a law enforcement officer. The district attorney is a representative of the state, especially in his activity as a public prosecutor, and legal provision is made for his supervision by the attorney general, who coöperates with him, and in certain instances supersedes him.

County law libraries are maintained and supervised by a board of five law library trustees composed of three superior court judges, the chairman of the board of supervisors, and a member of the county bar association appointed by the supervisors. Additional bar members are appointed in counties having fewer than three superior judges.

Fiscal Operations.—Control of county finances nominally resides in the county board of supervisors, but the actual organization for fiscal operations is generally dispersed among a large number of independent officers who participate in various phases of the fiscal process. County financial operations include budgeting, auditing, assessment, tax collection, and maintenance of the treasury. Annual budget estimates are prepared by the various spending officers and submitted to the auditor. He tabulates them in comparison with revenues and expenditures of previous years and submits this tentative budget to the board of supervisors. The board then holds hearings, revises the tentative budget, and approves a final budget which serves as an appropriation ordinance. In a number of counties chief administrative officers and administrative assistants, representing the boards of supervisors, exercise a degree of control over budget preparation as well as over the later expenditure of funds.

Expenditures of county funds are made solely on the warrant of the auditor, who must see that all disbursements comply with the requirements of the law and must prevent expenditures in excess of allowed amounts. Similarly money is received into the treasury only on the certificate of the auditor. He is thus able to maintain accounts of all money entering and leaving the treasury, as well as of any special funds that may exist. The auditor also makes a monthly examination of the treasurer's books.

The assessment of property within the county is handled largely by the county assessor, who performs this function for the county and for school and most other special districts, and who may do so for municipalities. All taxable property is assessed locally except that owned by public utilities, which is assessed by the State Board of Equalization and apportioned to the counties. Equalization of individual assessments may be accomplished by the board of supervisors, acting as a county board of equalization; this board may not, however, raise or lower the entire assessment roll of the county. The State Board of Equalization may equalize assessment rolls between counties. When local officials consider a property appraisal necessary, the assessor, the chairman of the board of supervisors, and the district member of the State Board of Equalization serve as a commission to conduct the appraisal.

Recent legislation gave the State Board of Equalization certain added powers over assessments and tax limits.[4] (1) The board must make an annual survey in each county to determine the average ratio of the assessed value of property to its true market value, both within the individual counties and for the entire state. (2) The board then adjusts the valuation of state-assessed property so its tax burden will be similar to that of other property in the county. (3) If a county's ratio is more than 10 per cent away from the state-wide average, the board may adjust the county's assessment roll to make it conform to the state-wide average. (4) County assessment ratios are also to be brought into line with the state average for the purpose of allocating state funds whose distribution is affected by assessed valuations. (5) In intercounty districts the tax rates in the various counties are to be adjusted so that all property in the district will bear the same burden in terms of its market value. (6) District tax limits are to be adjusted so as to permit as much revenue as the unadjusted limit would allow if the district's property were assessed at the state-wide ratio.

The principal responsibility for collecting taxes rests with the county tax collector, an elected official. It is his duty to collect property taxes and county license taxes. Other officers participate to a

---

[4] *Cal. Stats.*, 1949, chap. 1466.

County Functions and Finance

limited extent, with the assessor collecting certain unsecured taxes, and the treasurer collecting the state inheritance tax. Many of the county officers, including the recorder, clerk, sheriff, and law librarian, collect fees for services rendered. The auditor is responsible for the collection of state and federal subventions through the submission of claims or reports. All county money is deposited with the elective county treasurer, who has charge of the investment of surplus county funds. Money is generally received into or disbursed from the treasury on the certificate or warrant of the auditor. The function of the treasurer is thus largely clerical.

Electoral System.—The election system operated by the counties functions in the election of state and national as well as county officers. Detailed election procedure set forth in the Election Code is carried out by county and precinct officers appointed by the board of supervisors acting as a board of election commissioners. Election results are filed with the county clerk, canvassed by the board of supervisors, and forwarded to appropriate state and federal officials. There is little state administrative control over county management of elections.

Matters Affected with the Public Interest.—A number of special matters affected with the public interest are handled as county functions. These include (1) investigation of the deaths of persons suspected of having died of unnatural causes, (2) administration of estates for which arrangements have not otherwise been made, (3) provision of free legal services for persons unable to afford counsel, and (4) surveying.

The coroner holds an inquest when a death occurs from violence or under suspicious circumstances. In carrying out this function he may organize a jury of inquest, summon and examine witnesses, direct that post-mortem examinations be held, and secure the services of experts in order to obtain a scientific opinion or explanation of the cause of death.

The public administrator manages and disposes of the estates of persons dying intestate and without known heirs. The office is elective, and is frequently combined with that of the coroner. This appears to be a logical arrangement, since most cases handled by the public administrator first come to his attention through the coroner.[5]

The office of public defender may be established at the discretion of the board of supervisors, and may be filled by either appointment

---

[5] Alameda County Taxpayers' Association, *Alameda County Government* (1947), p. 119.

or election. The public defender is charged with defending individuals who are not able to furnish their own counsel. In the absence of this office the court appoints a member of the bar to provide defense in cases requiring it.

Surveying, defining boundaries, platting, and map-making are performed by the county surveyor, an elective official who must be a licensed land surveyor. In almost half of the counties, the surveyor has also taken over the duties of county road commissioner.

Recording.—The major record-keeping activities are performed by the county clerk, although the recorder does some of this work. The county clerk serves as clerk and record keeper for the board of supervisors, courts, board of equalization, board of election commissioners, and other boards. He issues marriage, hunting, and fishing licenses, and registers professional and legal documents deposited with him. The types of information kept by the clerk include a registry of voters, election returns, naturalization records, records of marriages, registers of persons engaged in professions concerned with public health, land titles, and records relating to county offices.

Purchasing.—Although in many counties the purchasing of supplies and equipment is done by the individual county officers and departments acting separately, under California law purchasing officers may be appointed and centralized purchasing systems established. The purchasing agent may provide three major services for all county offices and departments: (1) purchase of all materials, supplies, and other personal property, (2) rental of office furnishings and equipment, and (3) agreements with contractors to perform jobs costing not more than $2,000. County supply stores may be maintained within the purchasing department upon which the individual county offices may draw. A survey made in 1939 by the National Bureau of Standards indicated that 19 California counties had centralized purchasing.[6]

The centralization of purchasing makes possible the consolidation of requirements, quantity buying, standardization of specifications, and supervision of inspections. Purchasing can thus be done with greater efficiency by a central office, thereby relieving the regular county departments of responsibility for a nonfunctional "housekeeping" task.

Personnel.—In most counties personnel operations are handled on an individual departmental basis, each of the various county officers

---

[6] The 1950 roster of the California State, County, and Municipal Purchasing Agents' Association contains the names of twenty-eight county purchasing agents, indicating that some degree of centralized purchasing is now practiced in at least that number of counties.

County Functions and Finance

being responsible for the recruitment, selection, and employment of his staff. Salaries are fixed by the board of supervisors, but frequently with little semblance of county-wide uniformity for similar jobs.

A county may, however, through an ordinance approved by popular vote, adopt a civil service system applying to any or all nonelective officers and employees. A civil service commission of five members appointed by the board of supervisors administers the system, and provides for the classification of jobs covered, the formulation of pay scales, and the recruitment, testing, and certification of personnel. In home rule counties the charter may provide for the civil service system. Thirteen counties, excluding San Francisco, have instituted civil service systems.[7] Seven additional counties have adopted definite salary scales and job classification schemes for their employees.[8]

Employees of all welfare departments not covered by county civil service come under the county merit system. This system is administered by the State Department of Social Welfare, which approves compensation and classification plans, conducts an examination program, and supervises enforcement of merit system rules. The personnel standards of all county welfare departments in both civil service and non-civil service counties must conform to federal-state minimum standards required under the social welfare programs.

Significant steps have been taken recently toward the establishment of coöperative arrangements whereby counties provide personnel management assistance to cities, and whereby cities and counties may coöperate in administering tests, setting up eligibility lists, and conducting salary surveys. The State Personnel Board also assists various local governments, particularly in preparing test material, and in making surveys preparatory to installing salary and job classification systems.

Under a state enabling act counties may establish retirement systems, contributed to by both the county and its employees, for the provision of retirement allowances for eligible personnel upon termination of service.[9] Separate systems may be established for county peace officers and for county fire service employees.

Garages, and Buildings and Grounds.—Two final housekeeping functions of general government are maintenance of a garage to

---

[7] Alameda, Contra Costa, Fresno, Kern, Los Angeles, Sacramento, San Bernardino, San Diego, San Joaquin, San Luis Obispo, San Mateo, Santa Clara, and Ventura.

[8] Butte, Monterey, Orange, Santa Cruz, Sonoma, Stanislaus, and Tulare.

[9] *Cal. Gov. Code*, sec. 31200–32363.

service a central pool of county-owned vehicles, and the maintenance and operation of county buildings and grounds by a central engineering or janitorial staff.

Planning.—The use of the county as a unit of planning administration is one of the more significant recent additions to the list of county functions. Although planning as a local governmental activity has in the past been largely the province of municipalities, it has become increasingly evident that cities alone are unable to provide all the planning that is needed at the local levels.

First, because of geographic limitations, the authority of city planning commissions does not reach all urban or suburban areas requiring the conventional varieties of city planning. It is the county which must supply unincorporated areas with adequate subdivision and building regulation, zoning, and other planning aids. Second, in metropolitan areas there are many problems whose adequate solution requires the consideration of area-wide needs involving a number of separate city governments. The county planning commission (or the regional planning commission, which under present law is closely related to the county agency) is the logical unit to provide coordination and assistance in metropolitan planning.

Third, there are indications of an interest in planning and zoning of a rural and agricultural nature which might well become the province of county planning commissions.[10] Fourth, an awareness is developing of the need for the comprehensive survey type of planning which considers all the resources and potentials of an area, as well as the human, governmental, and other factors of the environment, and which attempts to chart the best routes for future development. In many instances this can be done most adequately when the county is utilized as the area for study.

The major activities of California counties in the planning field are subdivision control, land-use control, and master-plan preparation. Subdivision control, effected under ordinances passed by the board of supervisors and administered by the county planning commission, is intended to prevent the development of inadequate, overcrowded, and poorly planned subdivisions in unincorporated areas. Land-use control involves the zoning of areas within the unincorporated parts of the county, and has been devoted largely to the protection of property in urban and semiurban sections against the encroachment of undesirable uses. This type of control is also utilized through adoption by the board of supervisors of detailed sec-

---

[10] In Wisconsin, counties have zoned large areas of forest and cutover land against agricultural use and permanent residence.

County Functions and Finance

tions of the county master plan prepared by the planning commission. The county master plan may include provisions for conservation, land use, recreation, streets and highways, transportation, transit, public services and facilities, public buildings, standards of community design, and improved housing standards.

In connection with general planning activities, some of the more important work that has been done includes the planning of highways and airports and sewer systems, and the planning and location of new school buildings.[11] In addition, general surveys may be prepared of the human, mineral, and agricultural resources of all or part of the county with a view to guiding the future development of the area.[12]

A county planning commission contains five to seven members who are not officials of the county. They are appointed by the chairman of the board of supervisors with the board's approval. Additional advisory members are chosen from among the county officers, including the district attorney, the chief engineer or surveyor, and other officers, one of whom may be a supervisor. The advisory members have no vote unless specifically authorized by the board of supervisors. A county master plan, or parts of it, is adopted by a two-thirds vote of the commission after public hearings. The plan is then sent to the board of supervisors where its adoption depends upon a majority rule.

Regional planning commissions are legally required to be set up in order to facilitate coöperation among county and city planning commissions in areas having common interests and needs. At present, however, the only truly regional planning commission is found in Los Angeles County and is composed of the county planning commission in an ex officio capacity. A Tri-County Park and Recreation Planning Commission has, however, been established in El Dorado, Sacramento, and Placer counties. Its purpose is to plan for the development of a three-mile zone around the lake formed by Folsom Dam.

Urban planning commissions may be established by resolution of the governing bodies of cities and counties in which an urban area lies. Commission members are to be appointed from the respective city and county planning commissions by the chief executive officers of the participating governments. No such commission has yet been established in California.

---

[11] For a good illustration, see Santa Clara County Planning Commission, *Master Plan of Airports: Santa Clara County, California* (1948).

[12] A recent example is Riverside County Planning Commission, *Plans for the Coachella Valley* (1948).

PROTECTION TO PERSONS AND PROPERTY

County activities that provide protection to persons and property include law enforcement and maintenance of the jail, the recording of documents and information, the inspection of weights and measures, the provision of agricultural aids and livestock inspection, and fire, forest, and wildlife protection. Expenditures for protection were $36 million in fiscal 1949, or 7.2 per cent of total expenditures. Of this amount approximately one-half was devoted to law enforcement and maintenance of the county jails.

Law Enforcement.—County law enforcement activities, which affect the unincorporated area of the county, are carried on by the sheriff. It is his duty to preserve the peace, to investigate all public offenses in his jurisdiction, and to arrest wrongdoers. He is an officer of the county and has a number of duties related to civil and criminal proceedings, among them the summoning of jurors, and the execution of warrants, processes, and court orders. He manages the county jail.

Recording.—The county provides for the recording and preservation of documents and information designed to protect the property or personal interests of individuals. The county recorder's office, which carries on this function, handles legal documents, land titles, transfers, encumbrances, wills, and vital statistics. Certain other county recording activities related to the functions of general government are handled by the county clerk.

Testing of Weights and Measures.—The county sealer of weights and measures is periodically required to inspect and test scales, weights, and other measuring devices which are used in the sale of goods to the public; to measure packages of commodities for sale; and to test motor fuels. In the discharge of his duties he is subject to the general supervision of the State Department of Agriculture.

Agricultural Aids.—The county provides a number of aids and services to agriculture under the direction and supervision of the State Department of Agriculture. The county agricultural commissioner inspects orchards and nurseries, assists in the protection of orchards and crops from infestation, and works toward the abatement of plant and animal pests. Other county agricultural aids include the inspection of livestock, participation in agricultural extension service work, and control of predatory animals. In all of these activities the county acts in close coöperation with state agencies, chiefly the State Department of Agriculture and the School of Agriculture of the University of California.

Fire, Forest, and Wildlife Protection.—Rural areas are given

County Functions and Finance

county protection against fire, particularly forest, brush, or grass fires. This work is carried on in coöperation with the State Division of Forestry and the federal government, and only a few counties have the primary responsibility for forest fire prevention. County fire service may be extended to incorporated territory by contracts with municipalities; by similar agreements with the county, cities may furnish fire service to areas outside the city limits. A county may also provide fire service by means of county fire protection districts. These are organized to give additional protection to certain areas that are willing to pay a district tax. A few counties maintain a fish and game warden whose chief duty is the enforcement of state fish and game laws.

CHARITIES AND CORRECTIONS

This group of functions comprises the social welfare programs, activities of a county hospital and physician, provision of a home for the aged, and probation administration. Expenditures of $301,494,000 were made for these functions in 1949, sixty-three per cent of total county outlay.[13]

Social Welfare.—Four programs constitute the major social welfare activities of counties: aid to the needy aged, aid to the blind, aid to needy and crippled children, and general relief.[14] 1. Aid to the needy aged provides financial assistance to qualified elderly persons, with approximately ninety per cent of the costs financed by federal and state grants in fiscal 1948.[15] 2. Aid to the blind is provided under two types of assistance. The first, and by far the larger, is aid to the

---

[13] Includes $24,544,000 disbursed by the counties under contract with the state. State Controller, *Annual Report of Financial Transactions, 1949* (1950), pp. 274–275.

[14] During the period of operation of Article XXV of the California Constitution, the administration of old age security and blind aid was removed from the control of the counties and placed in the hands of the State Director of Social Welfare. The repeal of Article XXV, accomplished at the polls November 8, 1949 and operative March 1, 1950, returned the administration of the two welfare programs to the counties.

[15] Figures for old age security and the other social welfare programs were obtained from: Senate, Interim Committee on Finance and Taxation, *The Costs of Selected Governmental Services in California* (1949), Pt. 1. Since 1948 was the last full fiscal year of county administration of welfare before temporary changes introduced by Article XXV, financial information for that year has been used in preparing this section. The relative proportion of the burden borne by federal, state, and county governments is being maintained with only minor variations, since the return to county administration. The level of social welfare assistance payments, however, increased approximately 40 per cent between fiscal year 1948 and 1949. An additional 40 per cent increase was registered between 1949 and 1950.

needy blind, 80 per cent of the cost of which was provided by federal and state grants in fiscal 1948. The second type of blind aid is given to partially self-supporting blind residents, and is financed by the state and county governments only. 3. Aid to needy children is given to persons under eighteen who require assistance because of abandonment, or loss or incapacitation of parents. In fiscal 1948, 66 per cent of aid to needy children was furnished through federal and state grants. 4. General relief, financed solely by the counties, is made up largely of assistance given to indigents outside of institutions, and includes payments in cash, distribution of commodities, and provision of services needed.

The social welfare programs are administered either by the county boards of supervisors or by a board of public welfare, acting through welfare departments which have been organized in all counties. The first three programs, however, being supported largely from grants-in-aid, are subject to close administrative supervision by the State Department of Social Welfare which exercises supervisory, advisory, and reporting functions with relation to the counties. The department is also responsible to the Federal Security Agency for maintenance of uniform standards throughout the state and for the satisfactory administration of programs receiving federal grants. The state staff maintains a continuing relationship with the counties through regular visits to county offices. New policies are discussed and cases reviewed for compliance with state regulations, and for achievement of the general objectives of the assistance programs. The counties and the state also work together in developing policies and procedures to strengthen administration of the programs. A very significant aspect of this federal-state-local relationship is the supervision of welfare department personnel operations mentioned above.

County general relief, in contrast to the other programs, is exclusively the administrative and financial responsibility of the counties. The state Welfare and Institutions Code provides general guides and qualifications for relief eligibility, but specific regulations, determination of levels of payment, and actual administration rest with the counties. As a result the general relief program varies among counties to a greater extent than programs receiving federal and state funds. These latter programs are fairly uniform in coverage and amount of assistance.

An alternative system of administering general relief has been established by the Relief Act of 1945 which provides that upon resolution by the senate and assembly and declaration by the governor of an economic emergency the state will assist counties according to a formula based upon the property tax rate. Under this law the

County Functions and Finance

administration of relief would also be much more closely supervised than at present, with the possibility existing that the state could assume direct administration in counties which failed to comply with state regulations. Although by 1948 thirty-two counties had relief costs exceeding the minimum at which the state assistance could begin, the Relief Act has remained inoperative because there has been no declaration of an economic emergency.

Of the four social security programs, county general relief was responsible for the heaviest drain on locally derived county revenues in the fiscal year 1948, when $17,869,000 was spent. Aid to needy aged was next, with a $12,791,000 expenditure of funds originating locally. Aid to needy children and aid to the needy blind necessitated county outlays of $7,209,000 and $1,281,000, respectively. Total expenditures for the latter three programs are much larger; they are financed predominantly by state and federal aid. These three programs accounted for state, federal, and county outlays exceeding $140 million in fiscal 1948 and exceeding $200 million in fiscal 1949.

County Hospital and Physician.—Another major county function is the maintenance of a county hospital and provision of the services of a county physician for the care of indigents. Of fifty-three counties reporting in 1948, only two, Alpine and Mariposa, had no county hospital.[16] Only Alpine reported no expenditure for county hospital and physician's services in fiscal year 1949. Total expenditures for county hospitals and physicians in that year were $49,274,000.[17] Most of the necessary funds came from local tax sources; however, $3,190,000 was available from a state grant for care of the tuberculous.

County hospitals and other facilities for the care of the indigent sick are subject to a regular inspection and report by the State Department of Social Welfare.[18] The department also approves plans for changes in these facilities.

Homes for the Aged.—In 1949 only seventeen counties reported expenditures to provide homes for the aged. All counties, however, care for the aged in some manner. Frequently these expenditures

---

[16] State Department of Social Welfare, *Biennial Report 1946–1948* (1948), pp. 66–67.

[17] This does not include expenditures from state and federal allotments under the hospital construction program which provided $2,479,000 in 1949 for the construction and equipping of county, district, and private hospitals in California.

[18] Since 1947 the actual inspections have been made by the Department of Public Health by contract with the Department of Social Welfare. Responsibility for action on reports of investigations remains with the Department of Social Welfare. State Department of Social Welfare, *Biennial Report 1946–1948* (1948), p. 65.

appear in the budgets as items supporting the county hospital. Of the $5,989,000 reported to have been spent on homes for the aged in 1949, 80 per cent was disbursed in Alameda and Los Angeles counties.

Probation Activities.—Adult and juvenile probation work is an accepted function of county government in California. Adult probation, if properly carried on, involves the thorough investigation of offenders referred by the court, recommendations to the court regarding the disposition of their cases, and supervision when convicted offenders are released on probation. One of the major objectives of adult probation is to give the guidance of probation officers to those offenders who are most likely to respond to correctional treatment outside of penal institutions.

Juvenile probation involves similar work in dealing with juvenile offenders, plus an additional wide range of activities relating to children who may have committed no offense. The probation officer investigates cases referred to him of children allegedly dependent, neglected, abused, whose homes are unfit, or whose welfare is otherwise in doubt. If in need, these children will be given the protection of the court and the case-work services provided through the probation department. Consequently much of the work of probation officers with juveniles concerns children and youths referred to them for reasons other than the commission of specific offenses. Thus juvenile probation officers are active in the field of delinquency prevention as well as in the fields of correction and treatment. Additional activities of the probation officer include investigations in connection with the commitment of feebleminded persons, handling of money paid by court order for the support of a court ward, and management of the county's juvenile hall (detention home).

Probation officers are employed in all counties except Mono. These officers are nominated by the county probation committees and appointed by the juvenile court judges, except in counties having charters providing for other methods of selection. Probation committees, also appointed by the juvenile court judges, advise the probation officers in the administration of their departments and of the juvenile halls.[19] Expenditures for county probation work totaled $8,630,000 in fiscal year 1949.

Great inequities of probation department resources exist among the various counties, the more populous ones being better staffed and

---

[19] In Los Angeles County the probation committee is appointed by the board of supervisors. This committee actually has nothing to do with probation, and is responsible only for administration of the juvenile hall.

County Functions and Finance

equipped, and generally providing more adequate service.[20] An acute shortage of staff is to be found in counties of all sizes, however. No administrative processes serving to unify policies or performance in the separate departments are in evidence, except consultation service provided by the Youth Authority, and common endeavor.

Housing.—Counties may assist in the provision of low-rent housing to residents in need of it. A county housing authority is activated by resolution of the board of supervisors which appoints a commission of five members. Financial support is provided through federal, state, and local aid, and through the sale of bonds. Several counties now have active housing authorities which have developed some permanent low-rent housing, but the major part of their activity consists in the administration of temporary war and surplus housing disposed of by the federal government. A large part of the present tenant population is composed of veterans and their families.

HIGHWAYS

The counties maintain a road system of 65,076 miles in California, which is two-thirds of all the road and street mileage kept up by the state, cities, and counties. In the early part of this century the counties' funds for road maintenance were supplied predominantly from local tax sources. By 1949 a long-term trend toward state support of county roads through tax apportionments had resulted in the fact that nearly 84 per cent of the necessary money was provided by the state. Expenditures on county roads in 1949 were $58,205,000, of which state apportionments furnished $48,886,000 and federal aid $537,000.[21] The local sources of county road funds—taxes, traffic fines, and other general fund reserves—each provided about one-third of the remaining $8,782,000 spent on roads. County roads absorbed almost 12 per cent of all county expenditures.

Insofar as road expenditures are supported from taxes and special assessments, they may be made either a charge against the whole county, or a charge against specific districts or sections benefited. These special area levies may be made if the road concerned is not considered to be of general benefit to the entire county. The flexi-

---

[20] Special Crime Study Commissions on Adult Corrections and Release Procedures and Juvenile Justice, *Probation Services in California, 1948–1949* (1949), p. 43.

[21] State Controller, *Annual Report of Financial Transactions, 1949* (1950), pp. 230–231; idem, *Financial Report Concerning Streets and Roads of Cities and Counties of California, 1948–1949* (1950), p. 198. San Francisco figures are excluded, as well as those supporting federal aid secondary roads.

bility of locally derived road funds is limited, however, by the requirement that a major part of the return from road taxes be expended within the road district (supervisorial district) from which they were collected.

Until 1947 the administration of county roads, nominally vested in the board of supervisors as a body, was in most instances actually performed by each member of the board acting as road commissioner for his supervisorial district. Under this kind of management it was natural that standards of construction and maintenance, as well as highway adequacy, frequently showed large variations both between counties and between individual districts within a county.[22] In recent years, however, a trend developed toward centralizing all county road activities into a road department employing trained personnel and able to pool its equipment and conduct its planning operations on a county-wide basis. This trend culminated in a provision of the Collier-Burns Highway Act of 1947 which required such consolidation of the road functions in every county. All counties now have completed consolidation—although in a few instances the consolidation is only nominal—and a large majority of the road commissioners are registered engineers.

The Collier-Burns Act also established the principle of classification of county roads and the selection of a primary road system in each county for which a part of the state apportionments must be spent. Local authorities are allowed a good deal of discretion in making this selection and there is evidence that, although some counties have carefully chosen their primary systems, others have simply designated approximately one-half of their maintained mileage as primary.[23] All counties are now required to make comprehensive reports of road finances to the state controller who publishes annual compilations based on these reports.

Operation of the state highway system necessarily involves the state in relationships with the counties and with county road systems. Main intercity routes throughout the state have largely been designated as a part of the state highway system. The provision of minor connecting routes and feeder highways is predominantly the duty of the counties. In this way the state and the counties share responsibility for the development and maintenance of an integrated system of highways. The federal government is, of course, also involved in the picture through its expenditures on federal aid secondary roads,

[22] State Legislature, Joint Fact-Finding Committee on Highways, Streets, and Bridges, *Engineering Facts and a Future Program* (1946), p. 27.

[23] Senate, Standing Committee on Transportation, Subcommittee, *Report* (1949), p. 29.

County Functions and Finance

as well as through its support of the federal highway system. Although federal aid secondary roads are closely related to the county highway system, state and federal expenditures in their behalf, $7,612,000 in 1949, have not been included in this study because such expenditures do not appear on the county auditors' records.

HEALTH AND SANITATION

Services performed by local health departments are preventive rather than therapeutic. Thus with a few exceptions the aim of public health work is the creation of a healthful environment rather than the cure of specific ailments. There are six basic kinds of public health department activities: (1) the collection and use of vital and general statistics relating to health; (2) health education; (3) control of communicable diseases such as smallpox and scarlet fever, and others such as tuberculosis and venereal diseases; (4) provision of maternal and child health services for the education of mothers in proper prenatal and postnatal care and for the location, diagnosing, and therapy of crippled children; (5) environmental sanitation, including food inspection, control of food handlers, inspection of water supplies and sewage disposal facilities; (6) maintenance of laboratory services for bacteriological and seriological examinations relating to the control of communicable disease, to the purity of drinking water, to pollution of swimming areas, and to the sanitation of food and milk.

These are the six elements of a basic health program. Not every county makes them all equally available as there is considerable variance in both the quantity and quality of services offered by the local departments.[24] This variation is sometimes justified. For example, a small county cannot maintain a public health laboratory, but must contract for such services from other agencies. Similarly, larger jurisdictions go beyond the basic program and provide industrial hygiene and clinic services. Nevertheless, many differences in service are probably due to failures to change traditional forms of organization and methods of operation. Some counties merely employ a part-time health officer who is also engaged in the private practice of medicine. In several instances the position of part-time health officer is combined with that of county physician. It is largely in the rural areas, where part-time departments and traditional techniques continue to operate, that public health services are inadequate.

---

[24] Senate, Interim Committee on State and Local Taxation, *The Costs of Selected Governmental Services in California* (1949), Pt. 2, p. 26.

Recent scientific developments and recent state and federal legislation and subsidy have encouraged the development of full-time health departments. Forty counties possessing over 95 per cent of the state's population are now served by full-time units. It is felt that the subsidization of local health programs will bring further increases in the number of organized county health departments throughout the state.

There has been a significant development of the contractual exchange of public health services between counties and cities. Although every municipality is required to provide public health services, a large number have agreements under which they receive specified services from the county. In 1950 a total of two hundred and fifty cities in California had such contracts.

The State Department of Public Health confines its activities largely to supervisory and consultative relationships with local health departments. The development of some administrative control of local agencies by the state has been due partly to the fact that local health departments enforce the public health laws and regulations which are the ultimate responsibility of the state, and partly to the fact that the state department administers grants-in-aid derived from both federal and state sources. Eligibility for state assistance is conditioned on minimum personnel and organization standards which must be met by the local departments. These standards are adopted by the State Board of Public Health after approval by the California Conference of Local Health Officers, a unique organization in the field of state-local public health relations. In addition, the superior resources at the disposal of the department have enabled it to exercise leadership in the development of effective public health programs. Some types of direct health service are provided by the State Department of Health. Areas in which the local units cannot or do not supply certain basic services may receive them from the state. Specialized services that it is not feasible for each separate unit to maintain are made available by the department.

The payments of counties for health and sanitation amounted to $14,540,000 in fiscal 1949, approximately 3 per cent of total county expenditures. This sum was almost equally divided between the regular health service functions and care of the tuberculous. Funds supporting the health and sanitation functions come largely from the county, although state subventions supplied $1,431,000[25] for county public health services, and $3,190,000 for care of the tuber-

---

[25] State Controller, *Annual Report, 1949* (1950), p. 131. San Francisco excluded.

culous. The federal government contributed $446,000 to the county health agencies.[26]

EDUCATION

California counties perform three important educational functions in connection with local school systems. They serve the state government as an intermediate unit in the supervision of local school administration. They advise and assist the local school districts. They may occasionally make direct provision for emergency elementary schools or for certain other types of specialized training. Supervisory activities in which the county acts largely as an agent of the state include visiting, examining, and superintending the schools, and enforcing the course of study, the regulations for examination of teachers, the use of proper textbooks, and the use of uniform records and reports. The county superintendent of schools is also required to oversee the classroom instruction of elementary districts having fewer than 900 pupils in average daily attendance.

The superintendent's office provides local districts with assistance and specialized services that would otherwise be available only to the larger and wealthier districts. These services include audio-visual aid, advisory personnel placement, curriculum development and coördination, research and guidance, institutes for teacher education, health service, budgeting and financial counseling, school house planning, and school library services. Financial support for most of these aids comes from the county school service fund, which is a part of the state aid program. The state also pays $2,400 of each county superintendent's salary. Total state aid given to counties amounted to $4,702,000 in 1949.[27]

The county superintendent of schools may engage directly in the provision of emergency elementary education for the children of residents or migratory workers, as well as special classes and training courses for the physically handicapped and others. These activities are quite limited, however, for only 1,542 students throughout the state are receiving such instruction directly under the jurisdiction of the county superintendents.

County officers who are directly concerned with education are the county superintendent, who is generally an elected official, and the four other members of the board of education, who are appointed by the board of supervisors. The county superintendent is appointive

---

[26] State Department of Public Health, *California Public Health Report* (1949), p. 45. Includes payments to organized county health departments only.
[27] State Department of Education, *Apportionment of the California State School Fund, 1949* (1948), p. 88.

in two counties. The Los Angeles County board of supervisors and the Sacramento County executive appoint this official. The duties of the board of education consist largely of examining teaching candidates for certification, and preparing a course of study and lists of supplementary textbooks and standard supplies for the schools of the county. The major responsibility for educational activities at the county level rests with the county superintendent.

As another phase of their educational activities, counties operate public library systems primarily for the service of residents of unincorporated areas and small towns, the latter often contributing to the support of branch libraries. Book distribution is handled chiefly through small distribution centers; some counties also have bookmobile services. Books have thus been made available to many persons who would otherwise have had difficulty getting them. The Los Angeles County library has been outstandingly successful in this endeavor through its combination of highly centralized administration with regional decentralization and branch centers. Through contractual arrangements this library has also made its superior resources available to a number of cities and library districts.

In spite of many similar indications of success, however, county libraries generally have been criticized for several reasons. Because of limited financial support, their physical plants and book stocks are frequently quite inadequate to satisfy the need. There is much unevenness in distribution of funds and service, and there has been a failure to install effective administrative procedures integrating and simplifying the work of the branch centers.

Expenditures on all educational activities amounted to $5,083,000 in 1949.

RECREATION

Approximately one-third of the counties make significant expenditures for recreation facilities including parks, playgrounds, beaches, and camping and picnic grounds, but only 14 per cent of the counties operate organized recreation programs for the use of the facilities. Most organized recreation has been conducted in or near metropolitan areas with the result that while a few counties have extensive and well-distributed programs the remainder have achieved only limited developments. Seven county recreation departments or commissions (excluding San Francisco) provide year-round services and employ a recreation executive one-half time or more.[28] Los Angeles and Kern counties together budgeted 58 per cent of all

---

[28] State Recreation Commission, *Second Annual Report* (1950), p. 13. The Sutter County and Yuba City joint agency is included in addition to six county agencies.

County Functions and Finance

county recreation funds in fiscal year 1949. These budgets totaled $5,061,000. Although recreation districts are not considered as a part of county government in the technical sense, several unincorporated communities are served by recreation districts in eleven counties.

In a few cases where the county operates no recreation program of its own, grants-in-aid are made to other agencies. Desirable coöperative arrangements have been developed whereby counties can participate financially with other jurisdictions, usually cities, school districts, and recreation districts. Joint financial coöperation is particularly important since these several agencies provide the major part of public recreation facilities and programs in California.

FINANCE

Receipts.—The two major sources of county receipts are the general property tax and subventions from the state and federal governments. Until the depression in the 1930's the property tax was by far the most important of these two sources. It produced approximately 78 per cent of all county revenues in fiscal 1931, whereas state and federal subventions supplied only 12 per cent. Since that time the property tax has progressively declined in relative importance, and state and federal aids have risen. By 1949 the property tax was yielding only 42 per cent of total county receipts while subventions from the state and federal governments were providing 50 per cent. Total receipts for that fiscal year amounted to $500 million.

This pronounced change in the relative importance of the chief county revenue sources is primarily due to (1) the inability of the property tax alone to cope with rapidly increasing county expenditures which rose from approximately $100 million in 1936 to $475 million in 1949; and (2) the strong state and federal support of county administered social welfare programs. Other contributing factors are increasing state aid for county activities in the field of education, which are 92 per cent state supported, and state allocations of liquor license fees and motor vehicle "in lieu" taxes to provide 3.4 per cent of the funds supporting all county functions. County highway operations are financed largely by state assistance. However, this development occurred earlier than in the case of the other functions, for by 1936 county highways were already 85 per cent state subsidized. Health and sanitation activities also receive substantial support. Other minor types of state assistance include aid to juvenile homes and camps, apportionments to help pay the salaries of county veterans' service officers and county agricultural commissioners, veterans' housing allocations, reimbursements for the administration and care of adoptions, and aid for the inspection of agencies caring for the aged and children.

The federal government is the source of approximately one-third of all aids to counties from other governments. Federal aid is concentrated almost exclusively upon social welfare, 98 per cent going to support that function, the remainder being devoted to highways, health, and the support of general government. State assistance is not so heavily concentrated on one function, although social welfare is still emphasized. Sixty-two per cent of state assistance went to social welfare in fiscal year 1949, 2.5 per cent to highways, 9 per cent into funds supporting general government and protection to persons and property, and the remainder was distributed among education, health, and miscellaneous minor aid programs.

In addition to these regular aid programs, the state has provided a local postwar public works appropriation of $45,000,000 to assist counties in making needed capital outlays. One-third of this money is restricted to highway financing, and the remaining $30,000,000 may be spent for other types of public works as well as highways. An additional $9,875,000 has been appropriated to help pay for preparation of plans and acquisition of sites or rights of way in connection with these projects. A part of this sum has been made available to cities.

Notwithstanding the decline in its relative significance, the property tax has continued to be one of the two primary sources of all county revenues, and is the one primary source of revenues collected directly by counties. In 1949 the property tax yielded 86 per cent of all such local revenues.[29] Other local sources included fees and commissions, yielding 4.4 per cent of locally produced revenues; charges for special services, 2.8 per cent; fines and penalties, 1.9 per cent; licenses and permits, 0.9 per cent; and all others, 4 per cent.

Expenditures.—During the decade 1939–1949 county expenditures increased 181 per cent from $169 million to $475 million. Roughly seven-eighths of this rise was due to the combined influences of population growth and inflation, and the other one-eighth was probably due to increased per capita levels of county services.

County expenditures are profoundly affected by the social welfare programs which together with the other activities included under charities and corrections account for 60.4 per cent of all county outlay. The costs of general government absorb 12.5 per cent of county

---

[29] There is no specified limit on the county property tax rate. In 1949, however, the rates in most counties lay between $1.50 and $2.50 on each $100 of assessed valuation.

funds; highway and bridge expenditures, 11.7 per cent; protection to persons and property, 7.2 per cent; health and sanitation, 2.9 per cent; and all other functions, 5.3 per cent.

These figures are based on the expenditures of total county funds, both those collected directly by counties, and those received as aid from the state and federal governments. In order to examine the effects of the various costs as drains on strictly *local* county revenues, the amounts supplied by the other governments must be subtracted. (See table 12.)

TABLE 12

California Counties: Expenditure of Revenue Collected Directly

Function	Per cent
Charities and corrections	40.1
General government	20.3[a]
Protection to persons and property	12.3[a]
Health and sanitation	5.1
Highways and bridges	3.6
All others	8.9
Remaining unspent	9.7[b]
Total	100.0

[a] Based on the assumption that state and federal aids supporting the county general funds (motor vehicle "in lieu" tax and liquor-license fee apportionments, and federal apportionments from flood-control lands, grazing lands, and forest preserves) are finally spent two-thirds on general governmental functions and one-third on protection to persons and property.

[b] It is assumed that the amount by which county receipts in 1949 exceeded expenditures was composed wholly of revenues collected directly by the counties, that is, that all money received from other governments was spent.

Despite state and federal support, charities and corrections still constitute the heaviest single demand on revenues collected by counties. Expenditures for general government and for protection to persons and property require significant, although smaller, outlays. Health and sanitation and highways and bridges entail relatively small disbursement of strictly local funds, the first because its total expenditures are proportionately small and the second because it is supported largely by state assistance.

Bonded Indebtedness.—The bonded indebtedness of counties is controlled by constitutional and statutory regulations. A favorable vote by two-thirds of the qualified electors is required before a county can issue bonds.[30] In addition the total indebtedness may not exceed 5 per cent of the county's assessed valuation, except that debt concerned with water conservation, flood control, reclamation, irrigation, and similar projects may be allowed above this limit.[31] In any case, however, the total county debt may not rise above 15 per cent of assessed valuations.

County-secured indebtedness has declined markedly over a period of twenty years. Bonds to finance highway development have constituted the major part of county bond issues, and when the state accepted prime responsibility for supporting county highways in the 1920's, the counties were able to reverse a trend of increasing debt. In 1930 total county bonded indebtedness stood at $47,763,000 but by 1949 it had receded to $6,466,000, a decline of 86 per cent.

For specified purposes counties may now issue revenue bonds which do not constitute a liability against the county or the state, and which are secured only by the individual projects involved. The bonds are repaid out of revenues collected from project operations. Activities which may be financed in this manner include development of public beaches and small-boat harbors, and the construction and operation of county incinerators. A county board of supervisors may issue revenue bonds on simple resolution, with the qualification that such financing of beaches or boat harbors must be certified by the California Districts Securities Commission.

---

[30] *Cal. Const.* (1946), Art. IX, sec. 18.
[31] *Cal. Gov. Code,* sec. 29909.

CHAPTER VII

Special Districts: Characteristics and Patterns

The term "special district" or "special unit of government" applies to any local governmental entity which is neither city, county, township, nor village.[1] Usually a special district has (1) a resident population occupying a defined area, (2) a legally authorized governing body, (3) a separate legal identity, (4) the power to provide certain public services, and (5) a substantial degree of autonomy, including power to raise at least a part of its own revenue.[2]

These units have a variety of names: district, authority, *ad hoc* authority, and special district. In California, they are generally known by the last term. In power and legal status, they range from special assessment and improvement districts that are adjuncts of cities and counties, to large metropolitan districts that in jurisdiction are almost always larger than a city and frequently bigger than a county. Collectively, district activities include practically all urban functions, as well as a number of predominantly rural governmental activities.

The special district is a nationwide feature of local government in the United States. Every state possesses at least a few types. Furthermore, in the United States special districts are easily the most prevalent kind of local governmental unit and outnumber the combined total of all other governments. They are most frequently found in the newer states and those of recent rapid growth; the older states of the Atlantic Coast and the South have relatively few.

California uses the special district device more often than most states. If school districts are excluded, California is exceeded only by

---

[1] California townships do not have the attributes of local governments and are important only as election and judicial divisions. Villages are not part of the local governmental system in California.

[2] Not all special districts possess all of these characteristics. Some assessment and improvement districts are simply extensions of other existing local governmental units and receive no extended treatment here.

Illinois in the number and total expenditures of special districts.[3] As compared with its 304 cities and 57 counties, California has 4,356 special districts. There are thus more than twelve times as many special districts as there are cities and counties combined. The importance of special districts in fiscal terms is as fully evident as it is numerically. In 1949 these units paid out $505,136,000—a figure approximately equal to county disbursements for that year, and considerably above total city costs.

The nature of any special district is determined by the general or special state act under which it is organized.[4] Usually these acts carefully outline the kinds of areas that may be formed into a district, the procedures required for organization, the delegated functions and powers, and the composition and selection of the governing body. Methods of annexing area to the district and of dissolving the district are usually provided, and in a few cases the administrative structure is outlined.

ORGANIZATION PROCEDURES AND GOVERNING BOARDS

The first step in district organization is the circulation of a petition which must be signed by a specified number of qualified residents of the area to be included. Qualifications of petition signers vary with the nature of the district, but resident electors are usually eligible. However, when the needs of a particular group are to be served by the district, eligibility to sign may be restricted to those directly concerned.

The petition usually contains a description of the proposed district and an outline of the projects or duties to be undertaken. In some instances required tax levies or bond issues must be included. After being signed the petition is submitted to a local governing body, usually the county board of supervisors, which decides on the legality of the petition and holds public hearings on the proposed district. The discretion that the local governing body may exercise varies from simple determination of the legality of the petition to a decision on the necessity and suitability of the proposed district.

---

[3] U. S. Bureau of the Census, *Governmental Units in the United States, 1942* (1944), p. 9.

[4] Most districts are organized under laws of general application, but a few are provided by special act. Districts for irrigation, reclamation, and flood control may be created by special act (*American River Flood Control District* v. *Sweet* [1932] 214 Cal., 779). A special act creating an airport district has been held constitutional (*Monterey Peninsula Airport District* v. *Mason* [1942] 19 Cal. 2d, 446).

Special Districts

After approval by the local governing body, the organization proposal is usually submitted to a vote in the area concerned. A number of laws permit the district to be established by action of the local governing body alone, but most require an election. With a few exceptions all the resident qualified electors may vote. A simple majority vote is usually required to establish the district. The local governing body then passes a resolution that brings the district into legal existence.

Districts are governed by either (1) an independent elective board, chosen either at large or from subdivisions of the district; (2) an appointive board, generally chosen by the governing body which supervised establishment of the district; (3) an ex officio board, which consists of the county board of supervisors or the city council serving as governing body; or (4) a board composed of selected members of the governing bodies of constituent units. Many districts containing small areas, such as rural police protection and highway lighting districts, are governed by the county board of supervisors. Maintenance, local assessment, and improvement districts are administered by the city council or county board of supervisors. The largest districts, and those crossing local boundary lines, are usually governed by independent elective or appointive boards. The size of the governing body is specified in the enabling act. Three- to five-member boards are most frequent. In some larger districts the size of the governing body depends on the number of participating local governments and the populations involved.

POWERS, CHANGES IN AREA, AND DISSOLUTION

Special districts possess an array of general governmental powers common to practically all districts and shared by most other local governments, and the specific authority given to each district to perform the activity or activities for which it was established. The complement of general powers is substantially the same for all districts: the right of succession; the power to make contracts; to sue and be sued; to acquire and dispose of personal or real property; to tax and to float bond issues; and to hire employees. Other general powers that may be given, depending upon the nature of the district, are the right of eminent domain and the authority to adopt ordinances whose violations are punishable by law. Authorizations for specific district activity vary with the type of district. Activities are generally limited in each district to one or a few closely related functions. The services provided by various types of districts include a large number of the functions performed by the state, counties, and cities. A partial list of district activities includes public education,

TABLE 13

Number of Active Local Governmental Taxing Units in California, by Selected Years*

Type of governmental jurisdiction	Year 1935	Year 1941	Year 1950	Numerical change 1935–1950
Special districts	4,838	4,394	4,356	−482
School				
Elementary	2,951	2,539	1,827	−1,124
High	297	264	249	−48
Unified	...	40	61	+61
Junior college	18	14	18	...
College	...	...	1	+1
Acquisition and improvement— county	142	47	8	−134
Acquisition and improvement— municipal	120	59	25	−95
Airport	...	...	1	+1
Bridge	1	1	1	...
Cemetery	133	184	211	+78
Conservation—soil	...	2	28	+28
Conservation—water	6	10	18	+12
Drainage	15	17	13	−2
Fire protection	194	256	380	+186
Flood control	3	6	11	+8
Garbage	3	5	15	+12
Hospital	...	...	40	+40
Improvement				
Municipal	75	73	64	−11
Drainage	11	2	3	−8
Road	173	68	5	−168
Irrigation and water storage	95	104	104[a]	+9
Joint highway	10	12	13	+3
Levee	9	10	7	−2
Library	20	10	9	−11
Lighting	259	280	347	+88
Maintenance				
Lighting	59	59	54	−5
Road	...	...	1	+1
Sewer	...	49	107	+107
Storm drain	...	5	10	+10
Water	...	...	3	+3

TABLE 13 (continued)
Number of Active Local Governmental Taxing Units in California, by Selected Years*

Type of governmental jurisdiction	Year 1935	Year 1941	Year 1950	Numerical change 1935–1950
Memorial....................	...	...	18	+18
Mosquito and pest abatement..	24	27	41	+17
Park, recreation, and parkway..	2	9	49	+47
Police......................	4	5	9	+5
Port and harbor.............	2	4	15	+13
Protection and storm water....	8	6	9	+1
Permanent road.............	7	7	4	−3
Road, supervisorial..........	...	...	207	...a
Sanitary....................	51	79	115	+64
Sanitation..................	10	16	73	+63
Sewer......................	48	7	7	−41
Utility—municipal...........	3	6	3	...
Utility—public..............	16	29	51	+35
Water......................	68	78	117	+49
Miscellaneous (boulevard, local health, labor camp, mining, and county road).........	1	5	4	+3
Cities (including one city-county)..	281	285	304	+23
Counties (excluding one city-county)	57	57	57	...

* Sources: State Board of Equalization, Valuation Division, *Summary of Taxing Jurisdictions* (1950), and earlier reports; State Department of Public Works, Division of Water Resources, *Report on Irrigation Districts in California*, Bulletin No. 21-G, 21-M; 21-O (1935, 1941, 1943).

a There is no information available for reclamation districts, and no data for irrigation and water storage districts after 1943. Figures are available for supervisorial road districts for 1950, but not for 1935 and 1941.

bridge and highway construction, airport construction and maintenance, cemetery maintenance, fire and police protection, flood control, garbage and sanitation service, irrigation, water supply, park and harbor maintenance, recreation, and the provision of municipal utilities.

The relative importance of the various general functions handled by special districts is revealed by the distribution of expenditures. Districts handling the education function spend 92.2 per cent of all funds; protection to persons and property, 4.0 per cent; health and sanitation, 2.1 per cent; recreation and highways, 0.2 per cent each; and miscellaneous functions, 1.5 per cent.

Annexation of additional territory to an existing district requires the consent of the district and residents of the area to be annexed. Consent of the district is expressed through either a resolution of the governing body or an election, and approval of the annexed territory is given through either an election or a petition. Only a limited number of laws provide for consolidation of districts. Most consolidations must have an affirmative vote of the electorate in each district concerned. Some, however, may be effected simply through action by the county board of supervisors. In practically all instances the districts to be consolidated must have contiguous territories. More than one-half of all special district enabling laws include a dissolution procedure. These provisions are generally more stringent than the requirements for organization and frequently involve a petition, action of the governing body, and an election. In a number of the laws one or two of these three steps are omitted.

SUPERVISION AND COÖPERATION WITH OTHER GOVERNMENTS

Excluding school districts, approximately one-fifth of the special districts are directly governed by county boards of supervisors. Most of the other four-fifths, operating under their own governing boards, must have their budgets and tax levies approved by the county supervisors. It has not been determined to what extent these potential controls are actually used by the counties. There is, however, a trend toward closer administrative relations between many districts and the county. For example, in Los Angeles County the fire protection districts are managed by the county forester and fire warden, and their personnel organization is supervised by the county civil service commission. Purchasing for the county flood control district is handled by the county purchasing agent, and personnel by the county civil service commission. The county supervisors' association recently issued a manual of suggested procedure for those districts whose governing bodies are appointed by the boards of supervisors. The chief effect of this manual is to define and clarify the supervisors' budgetary and administrative controls over these units and to specify uniform precedures under which the districts are expected to operate.[5] A number of important districts are excluded from

---

[5] Harold Zenz, *Special Districts in California* (1950).

county budgetary control, and operate substantially as independent units. These include irrigation, reclamation, water conservation, drainage and levee, and mosquito abatement districts; school districts; revenue-producing utility districts; and intercounty districts of all types.

State controls over special districts are usually weak, consisting of mild supervision, or periodic reporting to a state agency. In a few instances state controls are fairly strong. Irrigation district finances and some phases of their physical affairs are supervised by the Districts Securities Commission, a state agency composed of the attorney general, state superintendent of banks, state engineer, and two district officials appointed by the governor. School districts are regulated through provisions of the education code and the state aid program.

The Bureau of Sanitary Engineering exercises permissive control over construction of sewage disposal systems. A permit for construction is granted if the system is found to cause no public nuisance or menace to health. Other districts subjected to varying degrees of state supervision include library districts (annual report to state librarian); reforestation and resort districts (preliminary plans must be approved by the state engineer); transportation districts (regulated by the State Public Utilities Commission); and regional planning districts (annual report to State Planning Commission, which is now defunct). Mosquito districts must file a record of their formation with the secretary of state. In addition, the State Department of Public Health takes an active interest in their operation, sponsors an annual conference of mosquito district officials, and furnishes them with free consulting services.

In 1933 the legislature enacted the District Investigation Act, requiring a comprehensive investigation and report upon proposed districts, with special attention to financial problems. The act has provisions designed to prevent the formation of districts in areas whose tax levels are excessively high, and to give owners of a majority of the property an opportunity to stop formation proceedings. This law applies to districts organized under twenty different specifically enumerated enabling acts. Primarily a depression measure, this law appears to have had little effect on district organization in recent years.

Another law, the District Organization Act of 1933, supplies a general form for the organization of districts, for annexation and exclusion of territory, and for consolidation and dissolution. The provisions of the District Organization Act become effective only if they are adopted in the individual district enabling act. The law has not achieved its purpose of obtaining uniformity in special district legislation.

A number of special districts are given definite authorization to engage in coöperative relations with other public agencies. Probably the most elaborate system for interdistrict coöperation is provided by the County Sanitation District Act of 1923. A number of county sanitation districts may work together in constructing and maintaining trunk sewers and treatment plans for their common use. A central organization may be established to do the administrative and technical work of all the districts. In addition, these districts may join with any other district, city, or other local governmental agency in building and operating sewage systems and disposal plants.

Under the Metropolitan Water District Act of 1927 public utility and local water districts may coöperate on a regional basis with each other and with cities in water procurement. This has been accomplished on an extensive scale by the Metropolitan Water District of Southern California. The Public Utilities District Act of 1921 allows a considerable degree of district joint action with counties, cities, and other local agencies in the construction and operation of public utilities. It also permits public utility districts to contract for services from other utility districts. The functions of sewage disposal and fire protection are frequently handled on a coöperative basis through contracts between districts, or between cities or counties and districts. Usually one agency undertakes to provide the service to other nearby smaller agencies. Similar techniques have been utilized by local library districts in contracting for books and staff services from county libraries, and by recreation districts in providing services in coöperation with cities, counties, and school districts.

Although more than 4,000 special districts organized under a hundred different laws and carrying on more than thirty distinct functions are active in California, several broad patterns are evident. They may be grouped into four major classes based on type of district function, scale of operations, and relationships with other governments.

1. Agricultural or rural districts serve rural areas, and their major activities do not substantially affect people living in urban centers. The chief functions of such districts are irrigation, reclamation, drainage, soil conservation, and water conservation. Most of them are independent of the county, and, if there is supervision, it comes directly from the state.

2. School districts are the most firmly established and best-known type of district. This is so because of their large number, volume of

Special Districts

expenditures, special relations with the county and state, and wide distribution.

3. Small quasi-municipal districts provide urban services to unincorporated communities. Among their services are sewage disposal, fire protection, police protection, water supply, mosquito abatement, parks, and cemetery maintenance. These districts may serve farm populations as well as urban communities, but the service is not primarily agricultural in nature as with the rural district. In some instances the needs of unincorporated areas are met by larger districts, such as a county-wide district, or by coöperating sanitation districts.

4. Large metropolitan or regional districts, such as the East Bay Municipal Utility District and the Metropolitan Water District of Southern California, are created to assist cities and smaller units to solve area-wide problems. These districts are usually characterized by large, well-defined administrative organizations.

AGRICULTURAL DISTRICTS

The most important agricultural districts are those concerned with irrigation, reclamation, drainage, soil conservation, and water conservation. They are all rural in nature, except those relating to water conservation, which may be used to provide a water supply for urban populations. Certain other districts (fire protection or police protection) may provide services for rural populations, but these are not strictly agricultural needs.

Irrigation and soil conservation districts are the most significant agricultural types. Soil conservation districts, most of which have been formed since 1941, are virtually independent of the county. Governed by five elected directors, their function is the furtherance of soil conservation activities and practices within their areas. Their formation is supervised, and their activities assisted, by the State Soil Conservation Commission. They also work closely with the national government in stimulating individual farmers to coöperation in soil conservation work. Important powers of this type of district include constructing improvements such as terraces for soil conservation, and regulating cropping and range practices subject to approval by landowners at an election.

The Irrigation District.—The irrigation district is the best and most important example of the agricultural district. One of the oldest types of district organizations in the state, it has had time to attain mature development and a well-defined position in the local governmental structure. Beginning with the Wright Act of 1887, the first law under which any important organization took place, the irrigation district has developed from an uncertain enterprise into a financially stable unit. In the ten years immediately following passage of the Wright Act, many districts were created, chiefly in southern California. Many encountered much difficulty because they were formed without sufficient consideration of water supply, agricultural potentialities, and financial ability to support the necessary irrigation works. Most of them were active only a few years.

Dissatisfaction with this first group of districts brought repeal of the Wright Act in 1897, and enactment of more stringent enabling legislation. A two-thirds vote for organization was substituted for the simple majority. In the calling of a bond election, petition by a majority of the landowners, who own more than one-half of the land area, replaced action by the board of directors. These changes in the irrigation district law resulted in a complete cessation of district organization for approximately ten years.

A second surge of district organization materialized during World War I and the 1920's when about a hundred new districts were established. Factors generating this new development were high agricultural prices, increasing population influx into California, and renewed confidence in the district form of organization. These districts were considerably more successful than their predecessors. The improved economic situation and the requirement that there be state approval of organization plans and bond issues undoubtedly contributed to this success.

The crucial test for this second group of districts came with the depression after 1929. Extensive financial delinquency and defaulting on bond issues soon developed. The state took action when it became apparent that the districts individually were unable to cope with the situation. The Districts Securities Commission was created in 1931 to direct refinancing operations. Under state supervision, and with substantial assistance from the Reconstruction Finance Corporation, irrigation districts returned to a stable financial position during the 1930's. Their financial condition continues to be good.

The Functions of Irrigation Districts.—Easily the most important function of irrigation districts is the procurement and distribution of water for agricultural uses. This usually involves making arrangements for the water supply and constructing and operating canals and distribution systems, and frequently includes operating pumping lifts. The district must also apportion water among its members, and provide drainage to facilitate irrigation work. Most water procurement operations of irrigation districts are necessarily small. Where large regional developments are necessary to insure the water supply, as is common in the Central Valley, the irrigation districts must depend upon a state or national agency.

Special Districts

Irrigation districts may also purchase or generate electric power, provide for its transmission, and sell it in or outside of the district. Although only a few districts are using this function, the magnitude of their operations is considerable. Electric power sales constitute 10 per cent of all irrigation district receipts. An additional responsibility recently given to irrigation districts is that of coöperating with the national government in improving and operating airports and airport schools, if there is no other public agency able and willing to coöperate. An indication of the importance of district irrigation activities is reflected in the acreage involved. The total area of all districts equals approximately 3,500,000 acres, or 5,500 square miles, of which about one-half is irrigated crop land. To this area districts deliver about five million acre feet of water per year, an average of 2½ acre feet per acre of irrigated crop land.[6]

District Relations with Other Governments.—Except for the requirements of its formation procedure, the irrigation district is independent of the county. The county board of supervisors reviews formation petitions, holds hearings, calls and canvasses elections, and issues the final order establishing the district. After it has been established, the irrigation district operates independently under its own elected board of directors. It levies taxes, makes assessments and collections, and maintains its own treasury, all separate from the county.

State regulation of irrigation districts begins with the stipulation that the state engineer make a feasibility report upon each projected district before its formation proposal is brought to a vote. This report includes a thorough investigation of the district's financial, agricultural, and engineering practicability. If the state engineer reports unfavorably, a three-fourths majority at an election is required to organize the district. Through informal relationships the state engineer stops many incipient districts before they have reached the petition stage. Then too, if some alteration of plans would increase the feasibility of the proposed district, the state engineer will advise local leaders to make such changes.

Irrigation district bond issues must be approved by the Districts Securities Commission, and expenditures from approved bond sales must be made under commission supervision. The commission passes judgment on district contracts involving an increase in indebtedness and supervises district refinancing. Individual districts are required periodically to submit to this state agency detailed reports of their activities and financial conditions, and the status of the agricultural crop within their boundaries.

---

[6] State Department of Public Works, *Irrigation Districts in California*, Bulletin No. 21–O (1943), table 1.

Prior to the use of the United States Bureau of Reclamation water supplies, the only significant relations existing between irrigation districts and the national government involved Reconstruction Finance Corporation loans to financially distressed districts. By 1940 federal loans authorized for this purpose approximated $27 million. It is possible that a new relationship between irrigation districts and the national government will grow out of operations of the Central Valley Project. Water from this project, controlled by the Bureau of Reclamation, is now becoming available for use by irrigation districts in various parts of the state. The bureau appears unwilling to release water in any quantity without contracts assuring it a degree of supervision over district activities as they affect the use of such water. If these contracts are generally signed by irrigation districts, a direct relationship between the districts and the federal government will have been established.

SCHOOL DISTRICTS

In practice the school district differs in three ways from all other types of district organization. The need for functions carried on by the school district is not limited to certain areas, but is found throughout the state. There is no alternative type of organization that offers the same service. The volume of activities carried on by school districts in terms of dollar expenditures far exceeds that of all other types of districts combined.

Organization and Governing Body.—A number of different varieties of school districts are found in California. In most instances, separate districts operate at the elementary, high school, junior college, and college educational levels. There are some unified districts providing both elementary and high school education and occasionally junior college training. These unified districts, which are growing in number, are most common in urban sections of the state. In 1950 the distribution of separate districts operating at the various educational levels, and of unified districts, was as follows:

Elementary	1,827
High	249
Unified	61
Junior college	18
College	1

Within the general classifications of elementary and high school districts, there are several different types. Among elementary districts there are city, regular, joint, union, and joint union districts. Among high school districts there are city, union, joint union, and county

Special Districts

districts. For the most part differences between these various types are of minor importance, and relate to the method by which the district was formed or to the governmental situation within which it operates.[7]

Most school districts are governed by locally elected boards of trustees, but the boards of education in charter cities may be either elected or appointed depending on the charter provisions. High school districts and many elementary districts have five-member boards. Some elementary district governing boards have only three members. Within the legal framework set out in the state *Education Code* the governing boards have wide discretion in conducting school affairs. They hire and dismiss teachers and other employees; prepare the budget; issue bonds within the legal limits; select sites and authorize plans for school buildings in conformity with state requirements; select supplementary textbooks from state-approved lists; purchase supplies and apparatus; provide for instructional supervision; and in general make policy decisions determining the extent and adequacy of the school program.[8]

The school district tax is actually levied by the county board of supervisors, but since it is mandatory that the supervisors levy a tax sufficient to fulfill the requirements of the district budget, the effective taxing power resides in the district board. Tax levies that exceed established statutory limits require a favorable vote of district residents for approval. The exact limits depend upon the number of levels of education offered within the district:[9]

Level of education	Tax limit per $100 assessed valuation
Kindergarten	$0.10
Elementary school	0.80
High school	0.75
Junior college	0.35

---

[7] City districts are those operating in incorporated cities except cities of the sixth class. A regular elementary district is any single district other than a city district. A union elementary district is formed by combination of two or more contiguous regular elementary districts. A union high school district is one superimposed upon two or more separate elementary districts. Those districts with the word "joint" in the title contain areas in more than one county. A county high school district is a union high school district that contains all the area in one county.

[8] State Department of Education, *Study of Local School Units in California* (1937), p. 28.

[9] *Cal. Ed. Code*, sec. 6357.

The school boards may issue bonds only after a two-thirds favorable popular vote, and the total value of all bonds issued may not exceed 5 per cent of the assessed valuation within the district.

County and State Supervision and Assistance.—In California the county has been utilized as a unit of intermediary supervision by the superintendent of public instruction and the State Board of Education. The duties of the county superintendent of schools include visiting, examining, and overseeing the schools of his county; and enforcing the course of study, the use of proper textbooks, and regulations for the examination of teachers. He is responsible for collecting and transmitting to the state superintendent the attendance records, financial statements, and other records relating to school districts in his county.

There has been a significant development of the county superintendent's office as an agency providing the local districts with assistance and specialized services that would otherwise be available to only the larger and wealthier districts. These county services consist of audio-visual aid, advisory personnel placement, curriculum development and coördination, budgeting and financial counseling, schoolhouse planning, and school library services. These types of assistance are financed largely from the county school service fund which is part of the state aid program.

Public education is a state function, and, although the responsibility for immediate management has been largely delegated to the local districts, the state through its department of education exercises important supervisory powers.[10] State activities in public education include the provision of elementary textbooks, approval of high school textbooks, regulation of professional educational credentials and certificates, approval of high school and junior college courses of study, and adoption of rules and regulations for the government of public schools. Financial assistance given through the state aid program is a major source of local district revenues.

The detailed *California Education Code* contains general public school administration provisions relating to state and county administrative organization, local administrative organization, financial support, system of public instruction, courses of study, textbooks, employment and dismissal of personnel, admission, exclusion, and compulsory attendance of pupils, and environment and equipment. These code provisions establish a loose legal framework administered by the State Department of Education, furnish much oppor-

---

[10] State Department of Education, *Study of Local School Units in California* (1937), p. 23.

Special Districts

tunity for discretion on the part of the local districts, and allow a wide range in the quality of education provided.

District Annexation and Consolidation.—Annexation of one school district to another generally requires consent by petition or election of a majority of voters in the district to be annexed, and consent of the annexing district by action of its governing board. If the district to be annexed has become inactive because of small attendance, or if it is an elementary district not included within any high school district, action by the county board of supervisors is sufficient for annexation. The limiting factor in most consolidation or unionization proceedings is the requirement of majority approval by either parents or electors in each district that is included. The new program of optional reorganization relaxes this requirement.

School District Finance and the State Aid Program.—Major sources of California school district funds are the local property tax and funds provided by the state aid program. Small additional sums are provided by federal grants, and in a few cases by city appropriations. In 1949 total school district expenditures amounted to $427 million. Of this sum, approximately 42 per cent was provided by state aid, while 58 per cent came from the local property tax. Elementary school districts disbursed 51 per cent of all school expenditures; high school districts spent 28 per cent; unified school districts expended 17 per cent; and junior college districts used 4 per cent.

State financial assistance to local school districts is provided through six separate funds, each distributed on a different basis.[11]

1. Basic state aid provides $90 per average daily attendance of pupils within the district, with a minimum of $2,400 for any eligible elementary district. Average daily attendance is computed by dividing the total days of pupils' attendance by the total number of school days. High schools are given additional allotments determined by the number of years of study maintained. For the fiscal year 1950, $151,911,000 in basic aid was allotted.

2. State equalization aid is distributed in order to enable all districts to maintain a "foundation program" calling for annual district expenditures of $148 per average daily attendance in elementary schools, $185 in high schools, and $210 in junior colleges. In the fiscal year 1950, $34,051,000 in equalization aid was distributed.

3. Within limits, the excess cost of educating physically handicapped students, and 75 per cent of the excess cost of educating

---

[11] State Department of Education, *Apportionment of the California State School Fund, 1950* (1949).

mentally retarded students, is paid by the state. In the fiscal year 1950, $3,643,000 was assigned for these purposes.

4. The state assists in paying student transportation costs, the amount of assistance depending partly on assessed valuations within the district. Total transportation aid of $2,825,000 was given in the fiscal year 1950.

5. The county school service fund supports a number of activities through which the counties assist their school districts. The fiscal year 1950 amount was $4,989,000.

6. Legislation in 1947 and 1948 provided a fund of $55,000,000 to be distributed to impoverished school districts for the construction and improvement of their physical plants. During the fiscal year 1950 approximately $25,000,000 of this building-aid fund was disbursed. In 1949 a public school building-loan fund of $250,000,000 was established to give state assistance in the form of loans to districts, to be paid back on a sliding scale depending on the districts' other debt service requirements. The portions of such loans not paid back after thirty years are to be cancelled. Distribution of these loans began at mid-year, 1950.

The total of state aid for fiscal 1950 approached $223 million. The percentage distribution among the six types of assistance was:

Basic aid	68.2
Equalization aid	15.3
County school service fund	1.6
Excess costs of educating handicapped students	1.3
Transportation aid	2.3
Building aid	11.3
Total	100.0 per cent

Because of their large enrollments, elementary school districts receive the major portion of state aid. Their share amounted to 68.2 per cent in 1950. High schools received 24.4 per cent, junior college districts 4.9 per cent, and the county school service funds 2.5 per cent.

The state aid program, which is weighted to some extent in favor of the smaller school districts and those with low assessed valuations, consequently favors the rural districts. The extent of this weighting is apparent in a comparison of apportionments per average daily attendance unit of pupils in urban and rural counties. The four most populous counties—Los Angeles, San Francisco, Alameda, and San

Special Districts

Diego—received an average apportionment in the fiscal year 1950 of $109 per average daily attendance for elementary schools, and $111 for high schools. The five least populous counties—Alpine, Del Norte, Mariposa, Sierra, and Trinity—received $155 per average daily attendance for elementary districts, and $189 for high school districts.

A very pressing problem in the California state school aid program has not yet been solved. The conflict arises between the need to guarantee the availability of an adequate educational program in all parts of the state and for all residents, and the need to avoid subsidy and perpetuation of unnecessary districts which are too small to provide adequate education. Neither of these needs is being met in the current state aid program. The subsidy of inadequate districts has not given them an adequate educational program; it has, however, hindered their reorganization.

School District Reorganization.—California school district structure has two major organizational faults. (1) Elementary districts are exceedingly numerous, and a majority of them fall far short of recommended minimum attendance standards. Sixty per cent of California's elementary districts have an average attendance below 100. This is much lower than the 175 minimum attendance goal set by the National Commission on School District Reorganization. These inadequate districts predominate in rural areas of the state, and their presence usually means increased per pupil costs and lower educational standards.[12] The high school district situation is much better, since there are only one-eighth as many of them in existence; nevertheless, even if unified, more than 40 per cent of them would fall below recommended minimum attendance levels. (2) The segregation of different levels of education into separate elementary, high school, and junior college districts contributes to the excessive number and small size of districts, and obstructs the administration of an integrated educational program. Although these fundamental defects have long been recognized, California has only recently attempted a comprehensive reorganization.[13]

In 1945 the legislature created the State Commission on School Districts to supervise a state-wide survey aimed at planning effective

---

[12] National Commission on School District Reorganization, *Your School District* (1948), pp. 15–24; State Commission on School Districts, *The Effect of Reorganization of Elementary School Districts on School Costs* (1949), pp. 8–9.

[13] There has, however, been a long-term trend toward reduction in the number of elementary districts. Between 1937 and 1950 the number dropped from 2,710 to 1,827, a decrease of 33 per cent. (Based on information provided by the State Board of Equalization.)

district unification or reorganization wherever necessary. This state commission appointed five regional commissions, which in turn designated local areas for study and appointed local survey committees. The local committees, composed primarily of residents of the districts involved, studied their assigned areas and made recommendations in accordance with general policy outlined by the state commission. After local public hearings, and review and approval by the regional and state commissions, the reorganization plans were voted upon by residents of the affected areas. A favorable majority in the proposed district would effect a reorganization, except when a single district in the proposed district had a majority of all the voters. In that event two favorable majorities were required, one in the district having the most electors, the other in the combined area of all remaining districts. If the first plan was rejected, a resurvey was conducted, and the new plan voted upon not less than one year after the first election. After October 1, 1949 the duties of the state commission were assumed by the State Board of Education, the regional commissions were allowed to lapse, and the local survey committees, now provided for on a county-by-county basis, were appointed by representatives of the local school districts. Other phases of the reorganization program are being continued with little change.

The policy outlined by the state commission was phrased in general terms, and called for districts of sufficient size, population, and resources to offer an adequate educational program from kindergarten through secondary school.[14] In practice the reorganization effort has largely been directed toward the unification of existing high school districts with the elementary districts included within their boundaries. Such a unification program has its limitations, for many high school districts are of inadequate size. However, the achievement of comprehensive unification throughout the state would constitute a major improvement in district organization.

Most reorganization attempts have been defeated. Less than one-fourth of the proposals submitted to the voters since the beginning of the program have been approved. There are several reasons for the limited success of reorganization. Local pride, alarm over the loss of local control, and fear of increased tax rates are important factors. Equalization apportionments to unified districts would often be smaller than the total allotted to existing districts. The high value of rural real estate, and the higher assessment ratios frequently ap-

---

[14] State Commission on School Districts, *A Report on School District Reorganization in California* (1949), p. 23.

plied to it cause rural people to be apprehensive that they will bear an excessive share of unified school costs. The reorganization election provisions frequently operate to align rural against urban voters.

Several modifications in the reorganization program have been suggested.[15]

1. The final decision on a plan could be left to the discretion of the state legislature, a board, or a commission.

2. If the final decision on reorganization is to remain with the local electorate, it could depend upon a majority vote of the electorate in the total area. A number of plans in California have been defeated by an unfavorable vote in certain sections, although a majority of the total electorate approved.

3. State financial assistance could be so provided as to favor reorganization. Possible actions include increase in transportation aid, liberal school building assistance for reorganized districts requiring new facilities, reduction in district dependence upon the property tax, and a guarantee that reorganization would not mean a decrease in equalization aid. Oversubsidization of unnecessary small school districts could be terminated.

QUASI-MUNICIPAL DISTRICTS

An important use of the special district is to furnish municipal services to small communities that are not incorporated. These quasi-municipal districts may be used also as a means of coöperation between a city or cities and unincorporated territory. In such instances, the chief distinction between quasi-municipal and metropolitan districts is the smaller size and volume of activities of the former. Excluding school districts, this class contains the largest number of special districts in California.

Most quasi-municipal districts are small in area, their boundaries usually approximating those of the unincorporated community that they serve. Some include several communities or large unincorporated territories; a few are county-wide. Although they are distributed throughout the state, they are most numerous in suburban areas. Five counties, all of which have large suburban and fringe developments, contain one-third of the state's quasi-municipal districts.[16]

---

[15] National Commission on School District Reorganization, *Your School District* (1948).

[16] The five counties having the greatest number of districts (excluding school, irrigation, reclamation, and supervisorial road districts) are: Los Angeles, 341; Sacramento, 65; Orange, 84; San Mateo, 75; and Contra Costa, 67. State Board of Equalization, *Summary of Taxing Jurisdictions* (1950).

The most important functions that they provide to unincorporated areas are fire protection, street lighting, and sanitation. Other major district activities include cemetery maintenance, mosquito abatement, public health work, hospital construction, airport construction, police protection, and provision of a water supply. The most numerous quasi-municipal districts are fire protection, 380; lighting, 347; cemetery, 211; water, 117; sanitary, 115; and sewer maintenance, 107. Taken together, these six types account for almost 70 per cent of all quasi-municipal districts. In most instances each district provides only a single service.

Factors Causing Establishment of Districts.—There are a number of reasons for the creation of quasi-municipal districts. First, is the strongly felt need for a particular service. Second, property owners may fear that incorporation or annexation will mean heavier taxes than those levied by a special district. Third, solution of the problem through a municipal government may be impractical because of the small size and resources of the area, or because the problem may require coöperation between one or more small cities and the adjacent unincorporated territory. Fourth, if only a few services are needed, it may be felt that incorporation is unnecessary and uneconomical.

Government, Organization, and Annexation.—Most of these districts are governed by specially created bodies, either independently elected or appointed by the county board of supervisors. Some are governed directly by the county board of supervisors. The county board has legal budgetary control over a majority of the districts that it does not directly govern. However, the extent to which this control is used to influence district operations is not currently known.

The district governing body has authority to select all employees, to approve and pay bills, to authorize expenditures, and usually to request inclusion in the county budget of a property tax for district purposes. It may have the power to pass ordinances regulating affairs over which the district has jurisdiction. The directors or trustees generally take no part in actual district operation, although in some cases they perform clerical and inspectional duties. Most districts whose activities require full-time supervision are administered by a secretary, superintendent, or caretaker who is appointed by and responsible to the board of directors.

In some instances quasi-municipal districts governed by the county board of supervisors have been integrated into the county administrative structure. In Los Angeles County, fire protection districts are supervised by the county forester, lighting and waterworks districts

Special Districts

by the county mechanical department, sewer maintenance districts by the county engineer's office, park districts by the county parks and recreation department, and garbage districts by the county health department. This type of centralization appears to be successful, but its effective use depends upon the existence of a well-developed county administration. There is practically no state supervision of quasi-municipal district operations.

District organization procedure follows the usual steps of petition by residents, review of the petition by the county board of supervisors, and an election in the area. This procedure is sometimes modified to allow initiation by a city or county governing body instead of through the petition, or approval by one or more local governing bodies instead of through an election. Annexation of new territory requires the consent of the district governing body, and usually approval by residents of the area to be annexed.

Problems of Quasi-Municipal Districts.—Efficient, economical operation and improved standards are probably the greatest needs of those districts performing fire protection, police protection, cemetery maintenance, lighting, public health, and mosquito abatement services, all of which require small initial financial outlays. This does not necessarily reflect upon the interest or ability of present district personnel. An unpublished study relating to the San Francisco Bay area found most district directors to be motivated by a real community interest, and many district employees to have enthusiasm for their work.[17] However, the small scale of most district operations makes it difficult to obtain the advantages of purchasing in large lots, centralized bookkeeping, and personnel systems. Similarly, because of the limited need within a single district, equipment may stand idle when closer coöperation with near-by areas would result in fuller utilization. The contractual exchange of services between districts, between cities and districts, and between counties and districts represents a significant attempt to meet these problems. Direct supervision or administration of districts by the county government could be a means to the achievement of more economical operation and higher standards of performance.

Excluding the need for efficient operation, the chief problems facing districts requiring large initial outlays for sewage, sanitation, public utility, water supply, airport construction, and hospital construction are those of financing and planning their physical plant. The use of revenue bonds has helped these districts to meet their

---

[17] University of California, Berkeley, Bureau of Public Administration, "Survey of Local Governments in the San Francisco–Oakland Metropolitan Region," MS (1937), Vol. 7, pp. 31–32.

long-term financial problems, and the national government is assisting in the construction of hospitals and airports. The state is providing grants and loans for the planning and construction of several kinds of district facilities, and the State Bureau of Sanitary Engineering advises and assists in sewage planning.[18] In some instances, the counties are assisting with the planning of sewage systems, especially when the topography and other considerations call for coöperative action by several local communities.[19]

METROPOLITAN DISTRICTS

A number of special districts providing municipal services may be classified as metropolitan districts by reason of their large-scale operations, and because their services cut across numerous local governmental boundaries. There is no precise distinction between metropolitan districts and quasi-municipal districts. However, metropolitan districts are larger and contain one or more cities and unincorporated territory, while quasi-municipal districts are smaller and are generally found only in unincorporated areas. In some instances the same type of district is used for both purposes. The more important metropolitan districts are sanitation, municipal utility, water, bridge and highway, regional park, port and harbor, and airport districts.

Metropolitan districts are found chiefly in and near large population concentrations where there is need for coöperation by several cities to serve a common need. A typical situation that resulted in establishment of a district of this kind is exemplified by the history of the Metropolitan Water District of Southern California. A dozen cities in the Los Angeles metropolitan area, all feeling the growing need for an adequate water supply to supplement their failing resources, determined to combine forces in seeking a solution. The water district, established in 1928 for the purpose of procuring water

---

[18] As of December 31, 1949, allocations applied for by districts amounted to $4,498,000 for sewerage construction, $1,343,000 for flood control, $429,000 for hospitals and sanitariums, and $222,000 for fire protection. Other applications from all types of districts brought the total to $8,919,000. State Department of Finance, Local Allocations Division, *Report of Activities, December 31, 1949* (1949).

[19] Two examples of thorough sanitation studies made by county governments to aid local communities in planning integrated disposal systems are Santa Clara County, *Santa Clara County Sewage Disposal Survey* (1946), and Orange County, *Orange County Sewerage Survey* (1947). Both studies examine regional topography, sewage treatment and disposal needs, and types and costs of sewage works. Recommendations are made regarding sewerage construction and the organization of districts to carry out treatment and disposal plans.

Special Districts

from the Colorado River and transporting it to the Los Angeles area, now provides water for cities and water agencies in a three-county area running from Los Angeles to San Diego.[20]

Formation and Governing Body.—The formation requirements for metropolitan districts are usually less stringent than for most special districts. Also, more discretion and power in the initiation and organization of several of these districts is given to the cities and counties that are to be included. A county sanitation district may be established by a simple resolution of the county board of supervisors, unless there is a protest from 2 per cent of the voters, in which case an election must be held. Formation of a metropolitan water district is initiated by resolution of any city council, and is established by election in all municipalities whose councils have approved the resolution. Formation of a municipal utility district may be started by resolutions of one-half of the public agencies that are proposed to be included. A metropolitan fire protection district may be originated by any city council or county board of supervisors, and approved by the governing bodies of other cities or counties to be included.

In a number of cases, the governing boards of these districts are chosen so as to represent the governing bodies of local units that are members. The county sanitation district, for example, is governed by a board formed from city and county officials and distributed on a modified population basis. Metropolitan water district directors are appointed by the executive officers of the participating agencies. The governors of a bridge and highway district are appointed by the boards of supervisors of participating counties. In other instances, particularly when the district boundaries are coterminous with those of the county, the board of supervisors serves as the governing body. Municipal utility districts and regional park districts are governed by elective directors.

Supervision and Finance.—A number of these districts, such as revenue-producing utility districts and those operating in more than one county, are completely independent of county controls and their boards have the necessary powers for budgeting, assessment, and tax collection. There is little direct state supervision or control of these districts, other than the permissive control over dam construction, bridge construction, and sanitary system installation.

All of these districts have the power to levy a general property tax,

---

[20] Members of the district are Anaheim, Beverly Hills, Burbank, Compton, Coastal Municipal Water District, Fullerton, Glendale, Long Beach, Los Angeles, San Diego County Water Authority, Pasadena, San Marino, Santa Ana, Santa Monica, and Torrance.

but there is much variation in the extent to which this source is used. The Metropolitan Water District of Southern California receives more than 90 per cent of its income from the property tax, and the Los Angeles County Flood Control District depends solely upon this source. The East Bay Municipal Utility District, the Sacramento Municipal Utility District, and the Golden Gate Bridge and Highway District rely primarily upon service charges and toll fees. Because of their large resources, most metropolitan districts are able to float bond issues as easily as many cities. Their ratings in *Moody's Manual of Investments* indicate that the factors giving them financial security are considered adequate or high.

Merits of Metropolitan Districts.—The chief advantage offered by this type of organization lies in its ability to cross established governmental boundaries, and thus to provide a local governmental unit whose territory coincides with the area requiring its service. When the function is one needing unified, area-wide planning, the metropolitan district provides an agency through which this planning can be carried out. In addition, when the function requires a large capital outlay, the district pools the resources of governments that separately might be unable to finance the project. Because of its size, the metropolitan district makes possible the use of more effective and economical procedures in management, budgeting, purchasing, and personnel.

Possible Weaknesses.—The creation of a metropolitan district means the addition of a new governmental agency to the already unwieldy number found in most metropolitan regions. However, to the extent that it represents a concentration under a single head of a function that previously was distributed among several different jurisdictions, the district is an attempt to lessen the dispersion of authority. Under most district enabling acts, the preëxisting local governments vote as units either to be included or to remain outside the organization. The effectiveness and the regional nature of district planning and operations may be impaired if certain areas elect not to join. This possibility will never be eliminated so long as parts of an area retain a veto right which cannot be overridden by a majority vote of the entire area.

Certain metropolitan districts, such as the municipal utility district, call for the creation of an independent body of elective officials. A number of these districts have excellent reputations, but such independence is subject to two criticisms. (1) It increases the number of elective officials, and removes from the existing governments some of their powers and responsibilities. (2) The local governments that are to participate may be reluctant to relinquish control to the

Special Districts

district if they feel they are to have little or no influence on its operations. These last two difficulties could possibly be mitigated by provision always for representation of existing local governments on the district board of directors. County supervisors or city councilmen could sit on the district board, as in the county sanitation district, or they could appoint representatives, as in the metropolitan water district.

Bibliography

Adams, F. A. *Irrigation Districts in California.* Bulletin No. 2, State Department of Engineering. Sacramento, 1916. 151 pp.
———, *Irrigation Districts in California.* Bulletin No. 21, State Department of Public Works. Sacramento, 1929. 421 pp.
Alameda County Taxpayers' Association. *Alameda County Government.* Oakland, Alameda County Taxpayers' Association, 1947. 165 pp.
Bemis, George W., and Nancy Basche. *Los Angeles County as an Agency of Municipal Government.* Los Angeles, The Haynes Foundation, 1946. 105 pp.
Bollens, John C., and John R. McKinley. *California City Government.* Berkeley, University of California, Bureau of Public Administration, 1948. 69 pp.
Bollens, John C., Patricia W. Langdell, and Robert W. Binkley. *County Government Organization in California.* Berkeley, University of California, Bureau of Public Administration, 1947. 44 pp.
Bollens, John C. *The Problem of Government in the San Francisco Bay Region.* Berkeley, University of California, Bureau of Public Administration, 1948. 162 pp.
California, Commission on County Home Rule. *County Government in California.* Sacramento, 1931. 236 pp.
———, Commission on School Districts. *A Report on School District Reorganization in California.* Sacramento, 1947. 63 pp.
———, *The Process of Optional Reorganization of School Districts.* Sacramento, 1947. 77 pp.
———, Department of Education. *Study of Local School Units in California.* Sacramento, 1937. 137 pp.
———, Department of Public Works, Division of Water Resources. *Report on Irrigation Districts in California.* Bulletins, Nos. 21–21-O. Sacramento, 1929–1943.
———, Reconstruction and Reëmployment Commission. *The Administration, Organization and Financial Support of the Public School System.* Sacramento: 1945. 75 pp.
———, Senate Interim Committee on State and Local Taxation. *State and Local Government Finance in California.* Sacramento, 1947. 1,243 pp.
———, *The Costs of Selected Governmental Services in California.* Sacramento, 1949. 2 vols.
California Committee on State Organization. *Final Report of Committee on State Organization to the Governor and the Legislature of California.* Sacramento, 1941. 90 pp.
Crouch, Winston W., and Dean E. McHenry, *California Government.* 2d ed. Berkeley and Los Angeles, University of California Press, 1949. 407 pp.

Bibliography

Davisson, Malcolm M. *Business License Taxes, A Major Potential Source of Municipal Revenue.* League of California Cities Report No. 37. Berkeley, League of California Cities, 1945. 72 pp.

Holtzmann, Abraham. *Los Angeles County Chief Administrative Officer: Ten Years' Experience.* Studies in Local Government No. 10. Los Angeles, University of California, Bureau of Governmental Research, 1948. 77 pp.

Jones, Helen L., and Robert F. Wilcox. *Metropolitan Los Angeles: Its Governments.* Los Angeles, The Haynes Foundation, 1949. 224 pp.

Ketcham, Ronald M. *Intergovernmental Coöperation in the Los Angeles Area.* Studies in Local Government No. 4. Los Angeles, University of California, Bureau of Governmental Research, 1940. 61 pp.

Other studies in this series examine intergovernmental relations in public library services, fire protection, public personnel administration, planning, and health administration.

Kitchen, James D. *Administration of Municipal Sales Taxes in California.* Los Angeles, University of California, Bureau of Governmental Research, 1949. 50 pp.

Kroeger, Louis J., and Associates. *Administrative Organization and Practices, City of San Luis Obispo, California: A Report to the City Council.* San Francisco and Los Angeles, Louis J. Kroeger and Associates, 1950. 108 pp.

———, *Administrative Survey, City of Long Beach, California.* San Francisco and Los Angeles, Louis J. Kroeger and Associates, 1949. 10 vols.

Los Angeles (City), Bureau of Budget and Efficiency. *A Study of Local Government in the Metropolitan Area within the County of Los Angeles.* Los Angeles, 1935. 298 pp.

Public Administration Service. *City-County Fiscal Relationships in San Diego County, California.* Chicago, Public Administration Service, 1949. 32 pp.

———, *Organization and Management, City of Berkeley, California.* Chicago, Public Administration Service, 1945. 179 pp.

———, *The City Government of Lodi, California.* Chicago, Public Administration Service, 1947. 49 pp.

———, *The City Government of Oakland, California.* Chicago, Public Administration Service, 1948. 211 pp.

Rohrer, Margaret. *County Manager Government in California.* Sacramento, County Supervisors Association of California, 1950. 13 pp.

San Francisco Bureau of Governmental Research. *San Mateo–San Francisco Survey, 1928.* San Francisco, San Francisco Chamber of Commerce, 1928. 196 pp.

San Jose, City Manager. *Description of the Police Organization and Its Departmental Relations.* San Jose, City Manager, 1950. 28 pp.

Scott, Stanley, and John C. Bollens, *Special Districts in California Local Government.* 1949 Legislative Problems No. 4. Berkeley, University of California, Bureau of Public Administration, 1949. 38 pp.

Selig, John M. "The Chief Administrative Officer in San Francisco." Unpublished M.A. thesis. University of California, Berkeley, 1939. 183 pp.

Stromsen, Karl E. "Special Units of Local Government in California." Unpublished Ph.D. thesis. University of California, Berkeley, 1936. 256 pp.

University of Southern California, School of Public Administration, Delinquency Control Institute. *Current Practices in Police-Juvenile Relations.* Los Angeles, University of Southern California, School of Public Administration, 1949. 14 pp.

Zenz, Harold. *Special Districts in California.* Sacramento, County Supervisors Association of California, 1950. 9 pp.

Index

Administration, county. *See* County administration

Administration of justice: municipal, 31; county, 96

Administrative reorganization, county: under general state laws, 7; under home rule, 7; consolidation of offices, 73-75; effect of installation of staff activities on, 75; influences of new county functions on, 75; impact of supervisorial control of many county salaries on, 75-77; in Kern County, 77; in Stanislaus County, 77; under local county charters, 79-80; in Los Angeles County, 80-81; in Sacramento County, 80-81; in San Diego County, 80-81; in Santa Clara County, 80-81

Administrative reorganization, municipal: under general state laws, 7; under home rule, 7; activities of local groups, 8; in San Francisco, 88-89

Aged: aid to the needy, 105, 107; homes for, 107

Agriculture: county aids to, 104; county commissioner, 104; State Department of, 104; agricultural districts, 126, 127-130

Aid. *See* Federal aid; Intergovernmental relations; State aid

Airports, municipal, 41

Alameda County, 108; rejection of proposed city-county consolidation in, 9, 69; local charter, 79; appointed executive, 80 n. 31

Alviso, special charter in, 12

Appointment and removal authority, exercised by county appointed executive, 82

Annexation: failure of, 2, 10; legal requirements for, 59-60; reasons for, 60; territorial size of, 60; use in Los Angeles, 60; use in San Diego, 60; use in San Francisco Bay Area, 60; opposition to, 60-61; elements of successful programs, 61; in metropolitan areas, 63; in San Francisco, 63; to special districts, 124; to school districts, 133; to quasi-municipal districts, 139

Appointed executive: in Kern County, 77; in Stanislaus County, 77; in Alameda County, 80 n. 7; in Butte County, 81; in Fresno County, 81; in Los Angeles County, 81; in Sacramento County, 81; in San Bernardino County, 81; in San Diego County, 81; in San Mateo County, 81; in Santa Clara County, 81; specific limitations on powers in Sacramento and San Mateo counties, 86; interest in, 86-87; in San Francisco, 89

Areas, city, 8-11; basic problem of, 51; range of, 51; relation to population, 51. *See also* Fringe areas; Metropolitan areas

Areas, county, 9-10

Areas, special district, 8, 9, 55; changes in, 121

Assessment, tax: municipal, 30; functional consolidation of, 65; county, 98. *See also* Taxes

Attorney: city, 31; district, 97

Auditor: municipal, 30; county, 97, 99

Average daily attendance, defined, 133

Bay Area Aviation Committee, 36

Blind, aid to the, 105, 107

Bonds: municipal, 50; county, 118; special district, 121; irrigation district, 129; school district, 132

147

Borough government. *See* Consolidation
Bridges, functional consolidation of, 66-67
Budgetary control over districts, 124, 125
Budgeting: improvements in, 6; municipal, 30; county, 97
Building code, 39
Building management: municipal, 34; county, 101
Bureau of Reclamation, United States, 130
Bus systems, municipal, 43
Butte County: local charter in, 79; appointed executive in, 81

California Conference of Local Health Officers, 112
California Districts Securities Commission, 118, 125, 129
California Education Code, 132
Charities and corrections: financial importance of, 2; municipal, 44; county, 105-109
Charters. *See* Local charters
Chief administrative officer. *See* Appointed executive
Children, aid to needy, 106, 107
Chula Vista, recent adoption of charter in, 20
Cities, department of administrative management, 34
City-county consolidation: defeat in Alameda County, 9; periodic interest in San Francisco and San Mateo counties, 9; discussion in Los Angeles County, 10. *See also* Consolidation in metropolitan areas
City-county government. *See* San Francisco
City manager. *See* Council-manager form of government
City planning, 34
Civil service: municipal, 32; county, 101; county commission, 124
Clerk: in sixth class city, 15; city, 30, 34; county, 100
Collier-Burns Highway Act of 1947, 110
Commission form of city government: first use in United States of, 21-22; general abandonment of, 22; modified form in many small cities, 22-23

Commissions, municipal, 30
Common services, management of, 34
Community redevelopment agency, 42
Consolidated departments, municipal, 39
Consolidation in metropolitan areas, 67; San Francisco-San Mateo County discussions of, 67-68; Alameda County vote on, 69; of special districts, 124; of school districts, 133. *See also* City-county consolidation
Consolidation of county offices: permissible combinations, 73-74; extent of use, 74-75
Constables, appointment in certain charter counties of, 80 n. 7
Coroner, county, 99
Corrections. *See* Charities and Corrections
Council, city: in sixth class city, 14-16; in charter city, 17; legislative and executive functions, 29
Council-manager form of government, 4, 5; characteristics of, 23; principal functions of manager under, 23-24; formal differences from chief administrative officer plan, 24; comparison of use in California and United States, 24-27; reasons for growth, 27-28; abandonment of, 28; methods of installing, 28; executive function, 30
County administration: organization, developments in, 4; procedures and improvements in, 6, 95, 96; relations between districts and county, 124. *See also* Administrative reorganization, county
County finance, 97, 115-118
County functions, 1-3, 94-115; executive, 95; legislative, 95; justice, 96; fiscal, 97; administration of estates, 99; electoral, 99; free legal services, 99; investigation of deaths, 99; personnel, 100; purchasing, 100; surveying, 100; recording, 100, 104; buildings and grounds, 101; planning, 102; agricultural aids, 104; fire, forest and wildlife protection, 104; law enforcement, 104; testing weights and measures, 104; social welfare, 105; homes for aged, 107; hospital and physician, 107; probation, 108; highways, 109; housing, 109; health and sanitation,

Index

County functions (*continued*) 111; education, 113; library, 114; recreation, 114
County manager. *See* Appointed executive
County organization: under Constitution of 1849, 70; general law, 71-78; local charter, 78-87; differences in, 87
County sanitation district, 141; Sanitation District Act of 1923, 126
County school service fund, 113, 132, 134
County Supervisors' Association of California, 8
Courts: municipal, 31; inferior, 31, 96; reorganization, 31, 96, 97; superior, 96; juvenile, 108
Culver City, adoption of charter, 20

Debt limits: municipal, 49, 50; county, 118; school district, 132
District attorney, 97
District Investigation Act, 125
District Organization Act of 1933, 125
Districts, special, 119-143. *See also* Special districts
Districts Securities Commission, California, 118, 125, 129

East Bay Municipal Utility District, 69, 127, 142; general manager of, 5
East Bay Regional Park District, 69
Education: financial importance of, 3; aid from cities, 45; municipal activities, 45; county board of, 113; county activities, 113-114; California Education Code, 132; State Department of Education, 132; State Board of Education, 132, 136; state aid to, 133, 134, 135
Election commissioners, board of, 99
Election procedure: municipal, 31; county, 99
Electric power plants, municipal, 43
Electric power sales, irrigation district, 129
Electrical code, 39
Employee retirement benefits, municipal, 33
Equalization, State Board of, 98
Executive, appointed. *See* Appointed executive

Executive functions: municipal, 29; county, 95
Expenditures: county, 2, 116; municipal, 3, 49; special district, 3, 123-124

Federal aid, 3; to airports, 42; to urban redevelopment, 42; to housing, 44; to cities, 48; to public health, 113; to counties, 116; to quasi-municipal districts, 140
Federal aid secondary roads, 110
Federal Security Agency, 106
Federation. *See* Consolidation
Fees: municipal, 47; county, 99, 116
Fifth class cities, 14
Finance: local, 1-4; municipal, 46-50; county, 97, 115-118; school districts, 133; metropolitan districts, 141
Fines: municipal, 47; county, 116
Fire protection: municipal departments, 38; alarm system, 39; consolidated with police, 39; county, 104, 105
Fiscal operations: municipal, 30; county, 97-99
Forest protection, county, 104, 105
Forms of city government: mayor-council, 21; commission, 21-23; council-manager, 23-28
Freeholder charter. *See* Local charters
Fresno, only charter city operating under commission form of government, 22
Fresno County: local charter in, 79; appointed executive in, 81
Fringe areas: reasons for growth, 51-52; condemnation by city officials, 54; methods of acquiring services in, 54-55; utilization of study committee in, 56-57; incorporation in, 57-59; annexation in, 59-61
Functional consolidation: possibilities for, 10; health, 65; libraries, 65; tax collection and assessment, 65; bridges, 66-67; ports, 66-67
Functions: increases in, 1; similarity of, 1-2; county, 2; compared, 2-3; municipal, 29-46; county, 94-115; special district, 121, 123, 124, 127, 128, 138, 140

Garage: municipal, 34; county, 101
Garbage disposal, 41
Gas plants, municipal, 43

Gasoline tax subventions, 40
General law cities: virtually the same as sixth class cities, 14; list of new, 14 n. 3
General laws: organization of cities under, 14-17; discretionary appointive county officials and boards under, 71 n. 2; mandatory elective county officials under, 71; organization of counties under, 71-78; consolidation of county offices under, 73-75
Gilroy, special charter in, 12
Golden Gate Bridge and Highway District, 69, 142

Health. See Public health
Health Officers, California Conference of Local, 112
Highways, county, 109-111
Home rule: comparison of city and county, 7; beginning of comprehensive municipal, 12; significance to counties of, 78
Home rule charter. See Local charter
Hospitals: municipal, 44; county, 107
Housing authorities: municipal, 44; county, 109

Inactive cities, list of, 14 n. 3
Incorporation: failure of, 2, 10; legal requirements for, 57-58; extent of, 58; reasons for, 58-59; advantages of, 59; arguments against, 59
Indebtedness: municipal, 49, 50; county, 117, 118
Intergovernmental relations: state and federal subventions, 3; functional consolidation, 10, 65, 67; property assessment and tax collection, 30, 65; personnel administration, 32, 101; employee retirement plans, 33; planning, 36; airport aid, 42; urban redevelopment, 42; housing, 44, 109; education, 45, 113, 114, 132, 133-137; public health, 45, 65, 112; libraries, 45, 65, 114; recreation, 46, 115; subventions to cities, 48; joint efforts, 63-64; transfer of functions, 65-67; ports, 66; bridges, 66-67; fire protection, 105; welfare, 106, 107; county hospitals, 107; highways, 110; subventions to counties, 115, 116; county-district, 124; soil conservation districts, 127; of special districts, 124, 125, 126, 138, 139, 140; irrigation districts, 129; subventions to districts, 133, 140
Irrigation districts, 127; functions, 128; bonds, 129; state regulation of, 129

Jails, county, 104
Joint efforts. See Intergovernmental relations
Justice, administration of. See Administration of justice
Justices of the peace, election of, 80 n. 6
Juvenile control, 37
Juvenile probation, 108

Kern County, appointed executive in, 77

Law enforcement, county, 104
Law libraries, county, 97
Laws, general. See General laws
League of California Cities, 8
Lease contracts, municipal, 40
Legislative functions: municipal, 29; county, 95
Libraries: coöperative service of, 45; municipal, 45; county, 45, 114; functional consolidation of, 65; Los Angeles County, 114
Licenses: municipal, 38, 47; county, 100, 116
Local charters: illustration of home rule, 17; number of cities possessing, 17; procedure for city to adopt, 17; organization of cities under, 17-20; interpretation by courts, 18-19; benefits to cities from, 19; classification of contents of, 20; factors affecting success of failure of, 20; number of cities eligible to have, 20; recent adoptions of, 20; mandatory provisions for counties to include in, 78; procedure for county adopting, 78; organization of counties under, 78-87; in Alameda County, 79; in Butte County, 79; in Los Angeles County, 79; in Fresno County, 79; in Sacramento County, 79; in San Bernardino County, 79; in San Diego County, 79; in Santa Clara County, 79; in Tehama County, 79; optional provisions in county, 79; popular rejection in certain counties

Index

Local charters (*continued*) of, 79-80; county administrative reorganization under, 80-82; in San Francisco, 87-93

Los Angeles: territorial size of, 51; annexation by, 60

Los Angeles County, 108; Regional Planning Commission of, 64; local charter in, 79; administrative reorganization in, 81; appointed executive in, 81; Library, 114; Flood Control District of, 142

Managerial idea, influence in non-council-manager governments, 5

Master plan, municipal, 35

Mayor: election of, 21; selection from council membership, 21; in San Francisco, 88-89

Mayor-council form of city government: variation in, 21; executive function under, 30

Merced, recent adoption of charter, 20

Metropolitan areas: absence of comprehensive solution in, 10; growth of large special districts in, 11; number of, 61; growth of, 61-62; problems of, 62; transportation in, 62; elections in, 62-63; annexation in, 63; joint efforts in, 63-64; private planning in, 64; public planning in, 64; transfer of functions in, 65-66; consolidation and federation in, 67-69; regional special districts in, 69

Metropolitan districts, 69, 127, 140-143

Metropolitan Water District Act of 1927, 126

Metropolitan Water District of Southern California, 69, 126, 127, 140, 142; general manager in, 5

Municipal affairs, defined by court decisions, 19

Municipal Corporations Act of 1883, 14

Municipal finance, 46-50

Municipal functions: executive, 29; legislative, 29; fiscal, 30; electoral, 31; judicial administration, 31; personnel, 32; purchasing, 32; planning, 34; staff services, 34; police, 37; fire, 38; sanitation, 40; streets, 40; airports, 41; urban redevelopment, 42; public service enterprises, 43; charities and corrections, 44; health, 44; hospital, 44; public housing, 44; education, 45; libraries, 45; recreation, 45

Municipal organization: special charter, 12-14; general law, 14-17; individual charter, 17-20

National Commission on School District Reorganization, 135

Organization, county. *See* County organization

Organization, municipal. *See* Municipal organization

Organization, special district, 120

Parking meter receipts, 40, 48

Permits, municipal, 38

Personnel administration: improvements in, 6; municipal, 32; county, 100

Personnel Board, State, 33, 101

Physicians, county, 107

Planning: growing acceptance of, 6; municipal, 34; coördination, 35; in metropolitan areas, 64; county, 102

Planning commissions: county, 35, 103; municipal, 35; regional, 36, 103; urban, 36, 103

Plumbing code, 39

Police, 37; courts, 31; consolidated with fire department, 39

Port of San Francisco, 66

Ports, functional consolidation of, 66. *See also* Wharves, docks and landings

Powers and functions: of cities, 14-16, 19-20, 29; of counties, 70, 94; of special districts, 121, 123

Printing and duplicating, municipal, 34

Probation activities, county, 108

Property tax: local, 3; municipal, 46, 47; limitations on, 46, 47; county, 115, 116

Protection to persons and property: financial importance of, 3; municipal, 36-39; county, 104-105

Public Administration Clearing House, 8

Public administrator, 99

Public defender, 99

Public health: municipal, 44-45; functional consolidation of, 65; county, 111-113; State Board of, 112; State Department of, 112, 125

Public housing: municipal, 42, 44; county, 109
Public school building-loan fund, 134
Public service enterprises, municipal, 3, 43-44
Public utilities: State Commission, 125; District Act of 1921, 126
Public works: municipal, 34, 39-42; local postwar appropriation, 116
Purchasing: improvements in, 6; municipal, 32; municipal agent, 34; county, 100; county agent, 124; special district, 124

Quasi-municipal districts, 127, 137-140

Reconstruction Finance Corporation, 128
Recorder, county, 104
Record-keeping, county, 100, 104
Recreation: municipal, 45-46; State Commission, 46; county, 114-115
Refuse disposal, 41
Regional districts, 127
Regional Plan Association, 64
Regional planning commissions, 36, 103
Regional special districts, 69
Relief, 106, 107; Act of 1945, 106
Rent and sale of property, municipal, 47
Revenue bonds: municipal, 40; county, 118; special district, 139
Roads: central administration of, 109; county, 109; federal aid secondary, 110
Rural districts, 126

Sacramento County: local charter in, 79; administrative reorganization in, 80; appointed executive in, 81
Sacramento Municipal Utility District, 69, 142
Sales tax: county proposal for, 3; municipal, 47
San Bernardino County: local charter in, 79; appointed executive in, 81
San Diego, annexation by, 60
San Diego County: local charter in, 79; administrative reorganization in, 80; appointed executive in, 81
San Francisco: annexation in, 63; special legislative act of 1856, 87; administrative reorganization in, 88;

local charter of 1931 in, 88; mayor in, 88-89; appointed executive in, 89; miscellaneous officials and agencies in, 89
San Francisco Bay Area: Council, 36, 64; annexation in, 60; authorization for Metropolitan Rapid Transit District, 69 n. 11
San Francisco-Oakland Bay Bridge, 66-67
San Francisco-San Mateo Survey, 67-68
Santitary Engineering, State Bureau of, 125, 140
Sanitation: municipal, 40; county, 111-113
Santa Ana, example of a fifth class city, 14
Santa Barbara, abandonment of council-manager form of government in, 28
Santa Clara County: local charter in, 79; administrative reorganization in, 80; appointed executive in, 81
Santa Monica, abandonment of commission form of government in, 22
School District Reorganization, National Commission on, 135
School districts, 3, 5, 126, 130-137; aid from cities, 45; organization, 130; types, 130-131; governing bodies, 131; taxes, 131; supervision by county, 132; aid from county, 132, 134; annexation to, 133; average daily attendance, 133; consolidation of, 133; finance of, 133; unionization of, 133; State Commission on, 135; reorganization, 135-137
School superintendent, county, 132
Schools, the planning of, 103
Sealer of weights and measures, county, 104
Separation of powers, municipal, 30
Service charges, 3; municipal, 47; county, 116
Sewage disposal, 40
Sewer rentals, 40
Sheriff, county, 104
Sixth class city: major characteristics of, 14-15; clerk in, 15; treasurer in, 15; powers of councils in, 15-16; advantages of, 16-17
Social welfare, 3, 105; State Department of, 101, 106, 107; aid to blind, 105,

Index

Social welfare *(continued)* 107; aid to needy aged, 105, 107; general relief, 106; aid to needy children, 106, 107

Soil conservation districts, 127

South Gate, most populous general law city, 14

Special assessments, municipal, 40, 48

Special charter: Alviso, 12; Gilroy, 12; legislative interference under, 12-13; organization of cities under, 12-14

Special districts, 1, 3, 10-11, 119-143; regional, 69, 127; characteristics, 119; organization procedures, 120-121; governing bodies, 121; powers of, 121, 123; functions of, 121, 123, 124, 127, 128, 138, 140; annexation of territory, 124; consolidation, 124; dissolution, 124; budgetary control over, 124, 125; supervision by county, 124, 125; state control over, 125; four major types, 126-127; school, 126, 130, 137; irrigation, 127; soil conservation, 127; agriculture, 127-130; quasi-municipal, 127, 137-140; metropolitan, 127, 140-143; municipal utility, 141

Special laws, legislative interference with cities under, 13

Stanislaus County, appointed executive in, 77

State aid, 3; to cities, 40, 48; to airports, 42; to housing, 44; to public health, 112; to education, 113, 133, 134, 135; to counties, 115, 116; to quasi-municipal districts, 140

State Board of Education, 132, 136

State Board of Equalization, 98

State Board of Public Health, 112

State Bureau of Sanitary Engineering, 125, 140

State Commission on School Districts, 135

State Department of Agriculture, 104

State Department of Education, 132

State Department of Public Health, 112, 125

State Department of Social Welfare, 101, 106, 107

State employees' retirement system, 33

State legislative interference: special charters, 12-13; special laws, 13; reduction of, 13-14

State legislature: approval of city charters, 17; ratification of city charter amendments, 17

State Personnel Board, 33, 101

State Public Utilities Commission, 125

State Recreation Commission, 46

State Soil Conservation Commission, 127

Streets, municipal, 40

Subdivision control: municipal, 35; county, 102

Subventions. *See* Federal aid; Intergovernmental relations; State aid

Sunnyvale, recent adoption of charter in, 20

Superintendent, county, 113, 132

Supervision, exercised by county appointed executive, 83-86

Supervisors, county: in general law county, 71; in charter county, 78; comparison, 87; powers of, 95

Surveyor, 100

Tax limits: municipal, 46, 47; none imposed on county, 116 n. 29; school, 131

Taxes: county, 3, 115; municipal, 46-48; special district, 121, 131, 141; school, 131

Tehama County, local charter in, 79

Torrance, recent adoption of charter in, 20

Traffic control, 37

Transfer of functions in metropolitan areas, 65-67. *See also* Consolidation; Functional consolidation

Transportation, in metropolitan areas, 62

Transportation and equipment, municipal, 34

Treasurer: sixth class city, 15; municipal, 30; county, 99

Trinidad, least populous general law city, 14

Trustees, school, 131

Unionization of school districts, 133

United States Bureau of Reclamation, 130

Urban planning commissions, 36, 103

Urban redevelopment, 34, 42

Vallejo, abandonment of commission form of government, 22

Water pollution control, 41
Waterworks, municipal, 43
Weights and measures, testing of, 104
Welfare programs, proposed increase in participation by national and state governments, 3
Wharves, docks and landings, municipal, 43
Wildlife protection, county, 105

Woodland, example of a fifth class city, 14
Work week: police, 38; fire department, 39
Wright Act of 1887, 127

Youth programs, municipal, 37

Zoning: municipal, 36; county, 102

www.ingramcontent.com/pod-product-compliance
Lightning Source LLC
Chambersburg PA
CBHW021711230426
43668CB00008B/799